Scale 1: 500,000
or 8 miles to 1 inch
(5km to 1cm)

13th edition October 2011

© AA Media Limited 2013

Cartography:
All cartography in this atlas edited, designed and produced by the Mapping Services Department of AA Publishing (CE0061).

This atlas contains Ordnance Survey data © Crown copyright and database right 2013 and Royal Mail data © Royal Mail copyright and database right. All rights reserved. Licence number 100021153.

 Land & Property Services. This is based upon Crown Copyright and is reproduced with the permission of the Land & Property Services under delegated authority from the Controller of Her Majesty's Stationery Office, © Crown Copyright and database rights 2013. Licence No 100,363. Permit No. 130019.

 Ordnance Survey Ireland's National Mapping Agency © Ordnance Survey Ireland/ Government of Ireland Copyright Permit No. MP000913.

Publisher's notes:
Published by AA Publishing (a trading name of AA Media Limited, whose registered office is Fanum House, Basing View, Basingstoke, Hampshire RG21 4EA, UK. Registered number 06112600).

ISBN: 978 0 7495 7116 0 (paperback)

ISBN: 978 0 7495 7117 7 (wire bound)

A CIP Catalogue record for this book is available from the British Library.

Disclaimer:
The contents of this atlas are believed to be correct at the time of the latest revision, it will not contain any subsequent amended, new or temporary information including diversions and traffic control or enforcement systems. The publishers cannot be held responsible or liable for any loss or damage occasioned to any person acting or refraining from action as a result of any use or reliance on material in this atlas, nor for any errors, omissions or changes in such material. This does not affect your statutory rights.

The publishers would welcome information to correct any errors or omissions and to keep this atlas up to date. Please write to the Atlas Editor, AA Publishing, The Automobile Association, Fanum House, Basing View, Basingstoke, Hampshire RG21 4EA, UK.
E-mail: *roadatlasfeedback@theaa.com*

Atlas contents

Map pages	II
Road map symbols	1
Road atlas Britain 1:500,000 scale	2–65
Index to places in Britain	66–81
County, administrative area map	66–67
Mileage charts	68 & 90
Britain	68
Ireland	90
Road atlas Ireland 1:1 million scale	82–89
Index to places in Ireland	91–94

Map pages

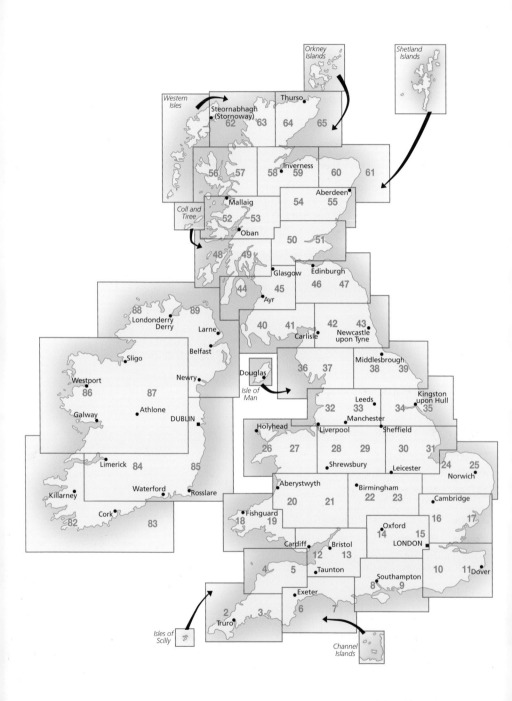

Road map symbols

Britain

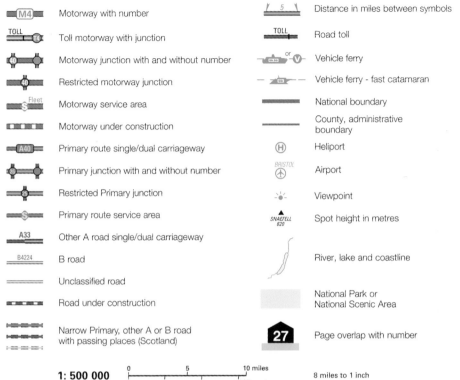

Motorway with number	Distance in miles between symbols
Toll motorway with junction	Road toll
Motorway junction with and without number	Vehicle ferry
Restricted motorway junction	Vehicle ferry - fast catamaran
Motorway service area	National boundary
Motorway under construction	County, administrative boundary
Primary route single/dual carriageway	Heliport
Primary junction with and without number	Airport
Restricted Primary junction	Viewpoint
Primary route service area	Spot height in metres
Other A road single/dual carriageway	
B road	River, lake and coastline
Unclassified road	
Road under construction	National Park or National Scenic Area
Narrow Primary, other A or B road with passing places (Scotland)	Page overlap with number

1: 500 000 0 — 5 — 10 miles / 0 — 5 — 10 — 15 kilometres   8 miles to 1 inch

Ireland

Motorway	Primary route (Northern Ireland)
Toll motorway and booth	A road (Northern Ireland)
Motorway junctions with and without number	B road (Northern Ireland)
Restricted motorway junctions	Distance in miles between symbols (Northern Ireland)
Motorway under construction	Minor Road
National primary route (Republic of Ireland)	Road under construction
National secondary route (Republic of Ireland)	International boundary
Regional road (Republic of Ireland)	Vehicle ferry
Distance in kilometres between symbols (Republic of Ireland)	Vehicle ferry- fast catamaran
Gaeltacht (Irish language area)	

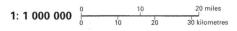

1: 1 000 000 0 — 10 — 20 miles / 0 — 10 — 20 — 30 kilometres   16 miles to 1 inch

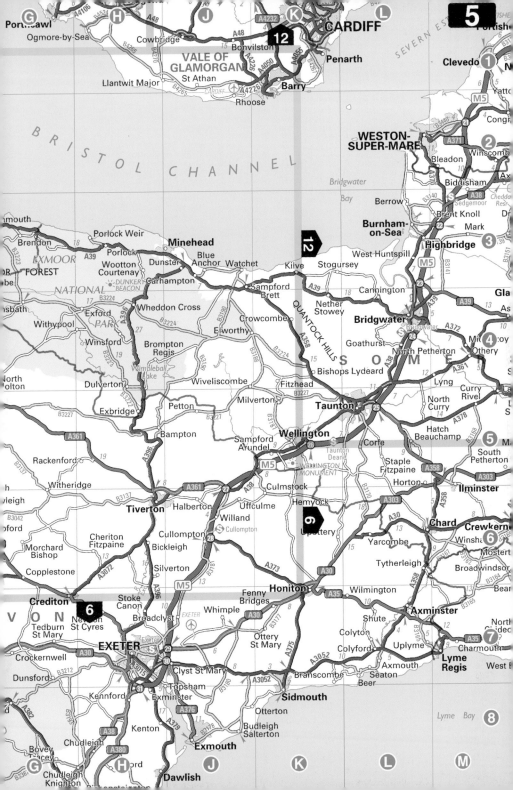

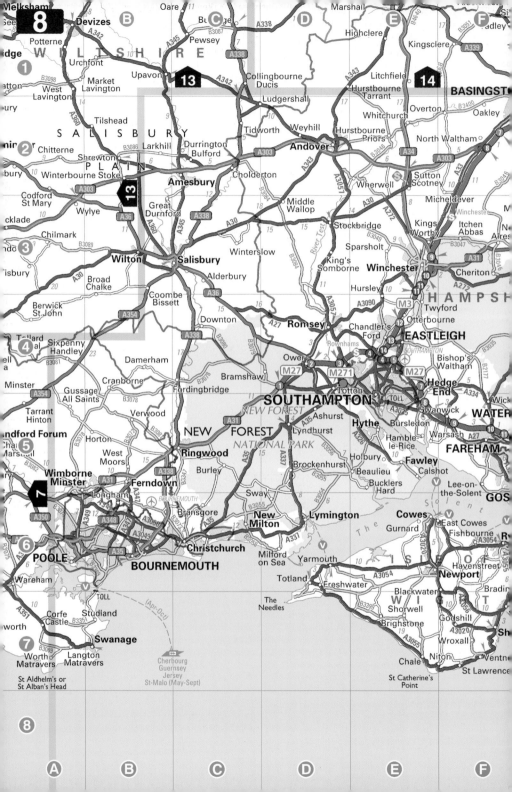

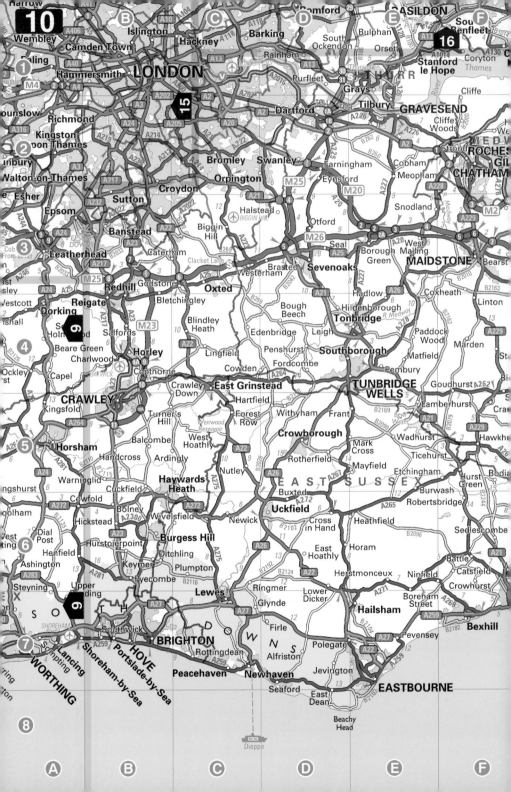

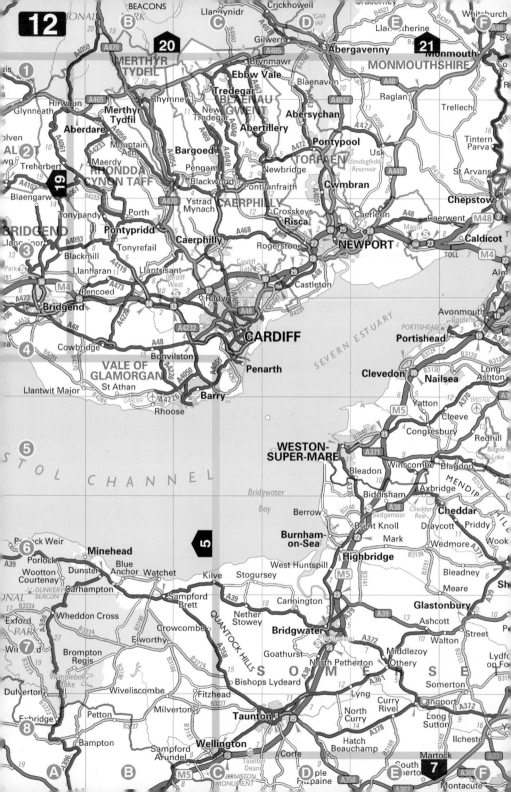

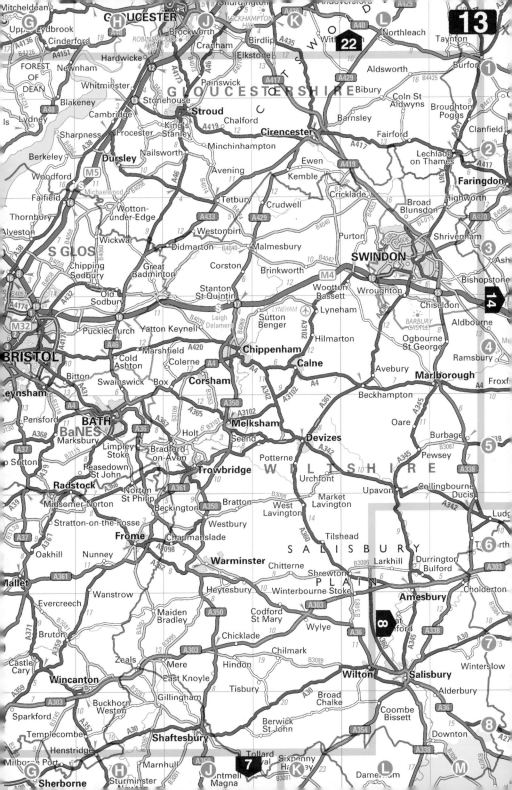

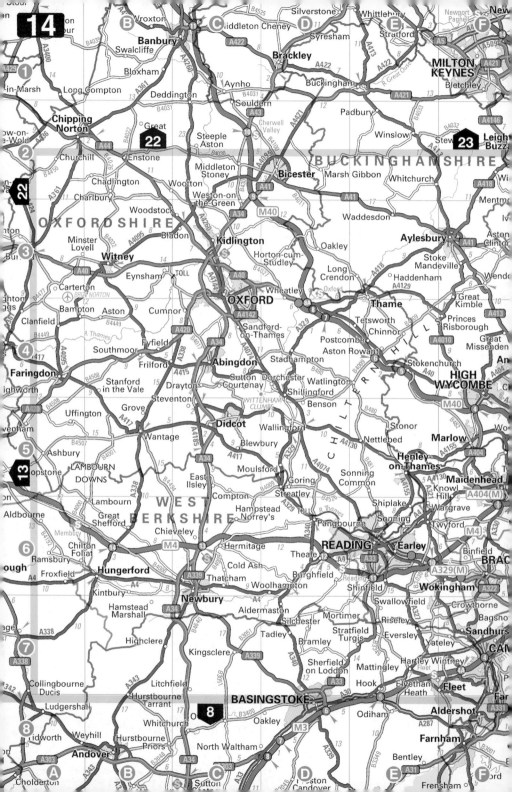

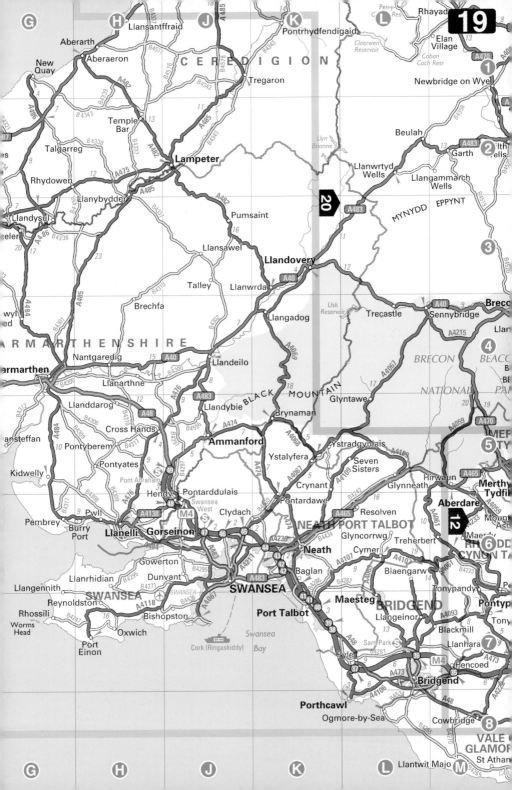

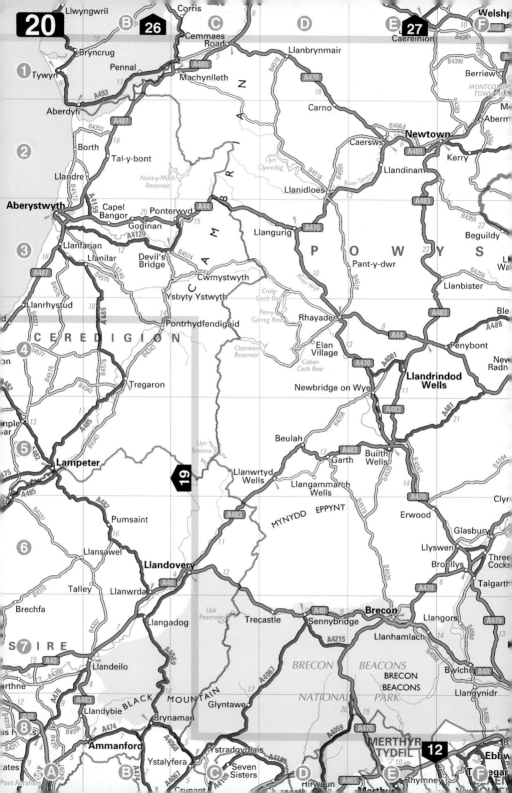

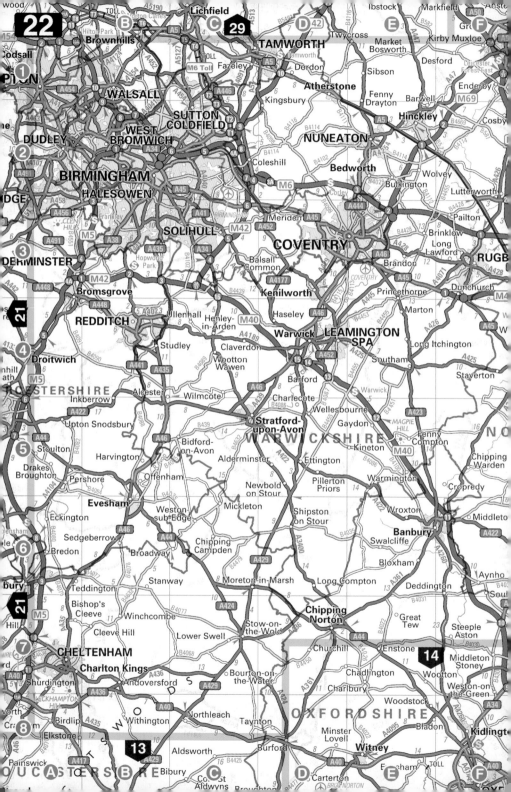

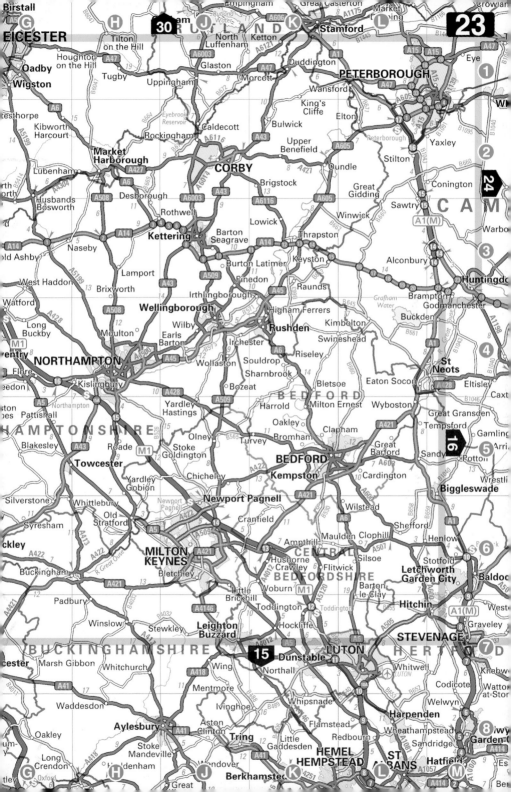

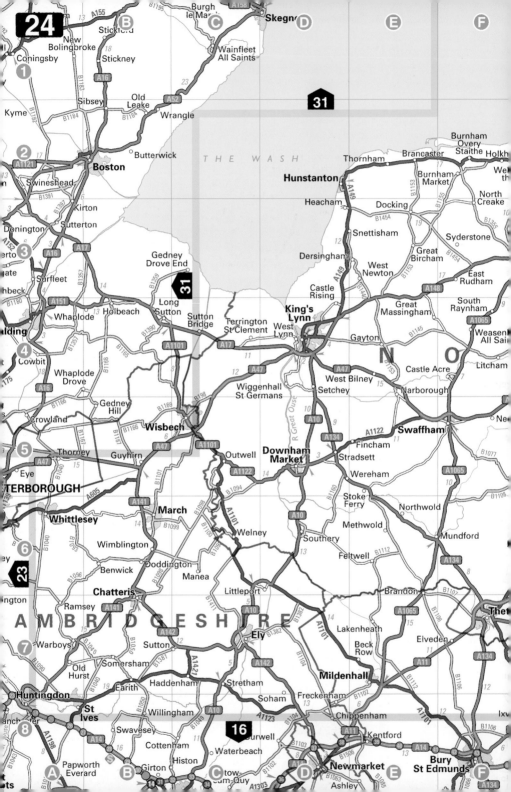

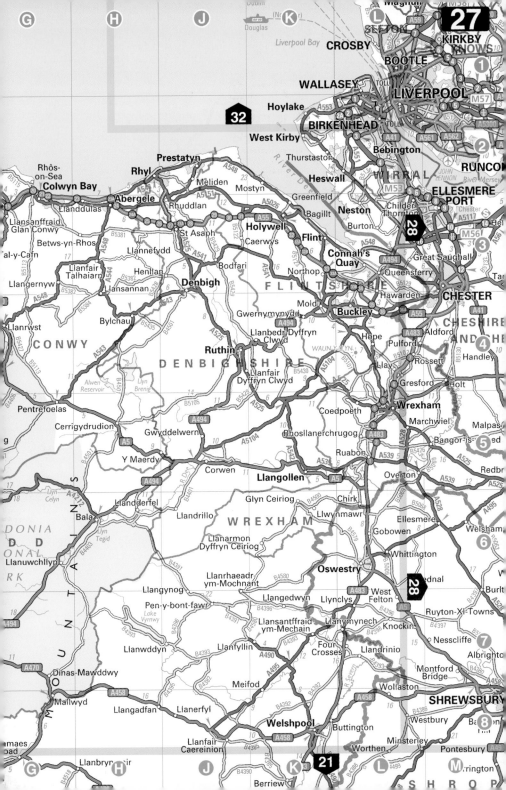

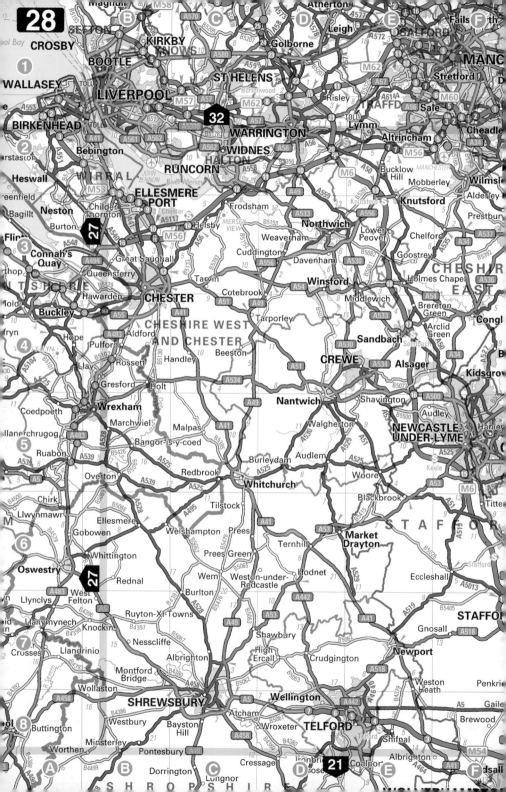

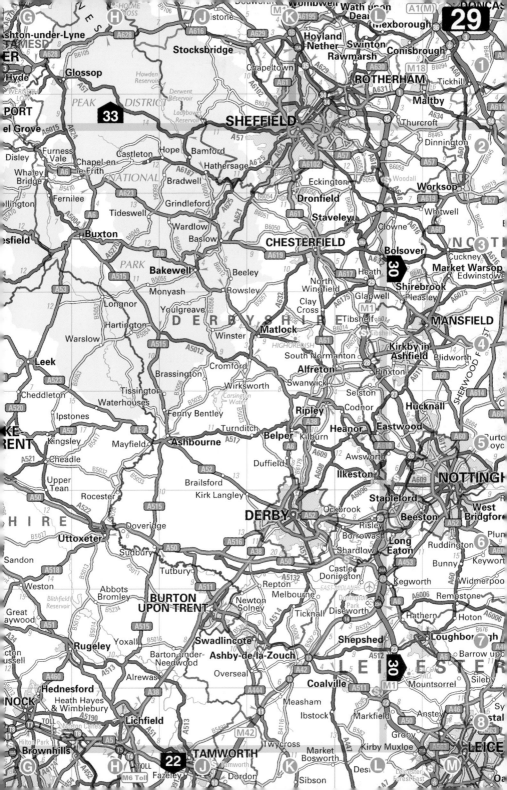

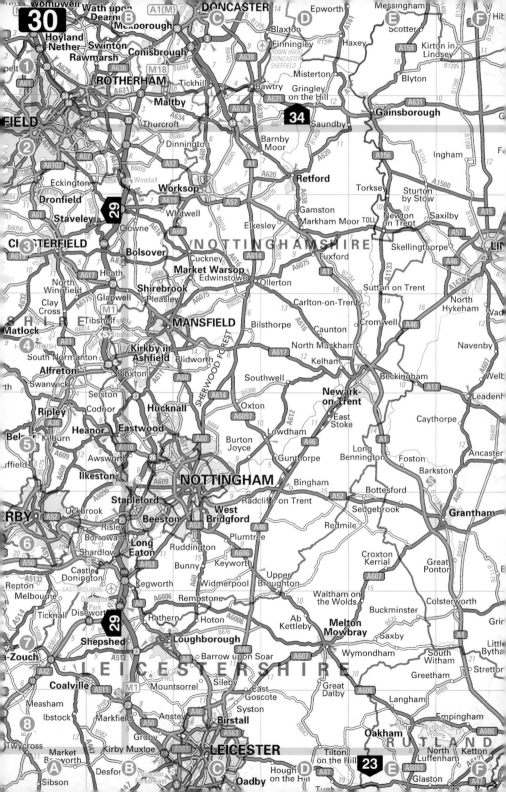

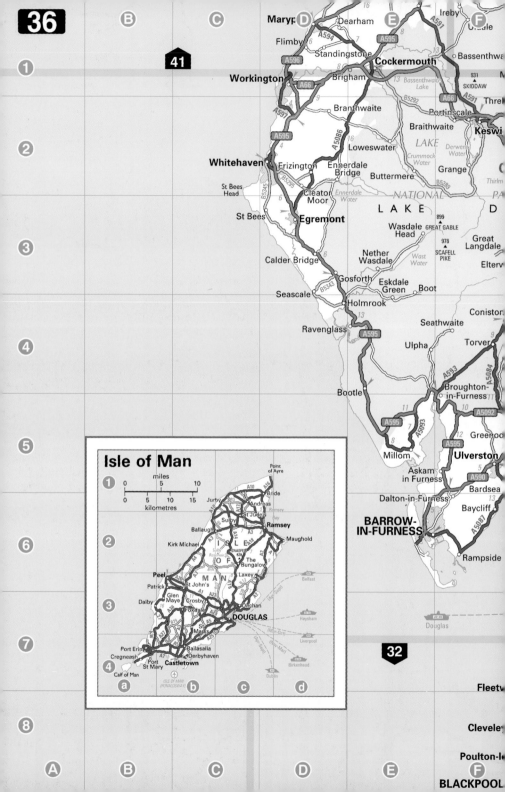

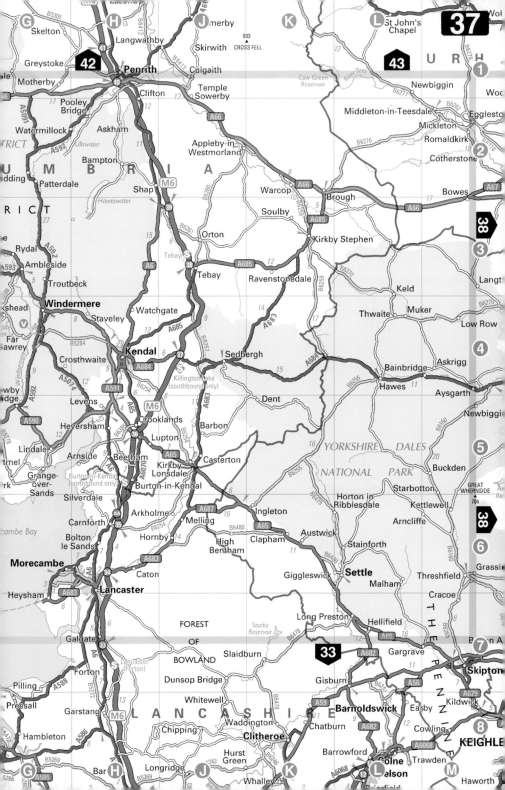

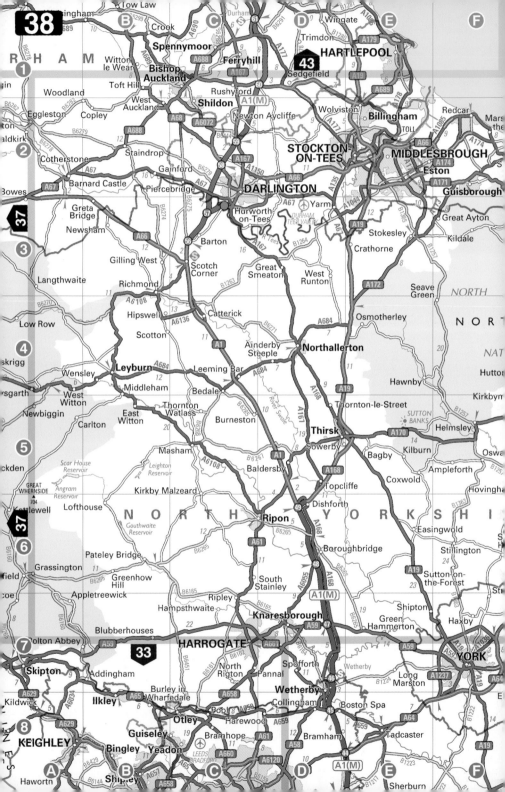

B C D E F

Ayr

1

Dunure
Alloway
Coylton
Ochiltre
B730
A70 7036
10

EAS
AYRSH
B7046

Maybole
Dalrymple
Kirkmichael
Patna
B741
A713
Dalmellingt
B742
Kirkoswald
Crosshill

Turnberry
Kirkoswald
Crosshill
Straiton
B741
Dalmellingt

2

44

A77
B741
SOUTH
Dailly
AYRSHIRE
Loch
Bradan
Loch
Doon
10

Girvan

Barr
A714

3
Lendalfoot 13
A714 8
Carsphair

A77
B73A
Pinwherry
9
MERRICK
842
CORSERINE
813
Colmonell
Loch
Moan
Loch
Enoch

Ballantrae
B7044
Barrhill
Loch
Dee
St
Larne (Mar-Oct)
Loch
Maberry
A714 22
Clatteringshaws
Loch

4
Larne
B7027
A712 19
Loch
Grannoch

Belfast
Stena Line to relocate from
Stranraer Autumn 2011
Cairnryan
17
New Luce
Newton Stewart
CAIRNSMORE
OF FLEET
710

Belfast
Kirkcolm
B738
A718
A75 15
Kirkcowan
7
Creetown
G

5
Leswalt
B7043
A75
Stranraer
A77
A716
8
Dunragit
A75 10
14
Glenluce
B7027
B733
Wigtown
A75 18

6
Portpatrick
B7042
Stoneykirk
B7004
19
A747
B7005
B7005
Kirkinner
Whauphill
B884
Sorbie
B7052
Garlieston
Wigtown

Sandhead
18
Mochrum
B7085
A746 11
B7063

7
Ardwell
Luce Bay
13
Port
William
B7021
Whithorn
10
Isle of
Whithorn
B7004

Port Logan
A716
Drummore
B7065
A747
Burrow Head

8
Mull of
Galloway

A B C D E F

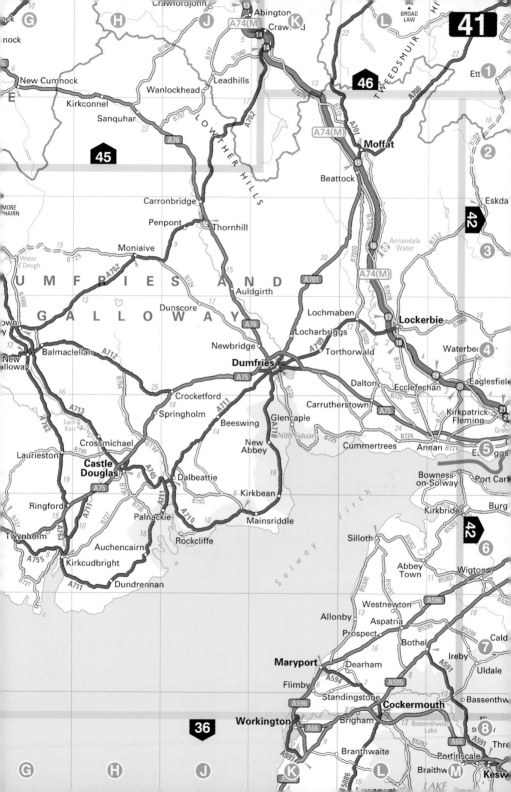

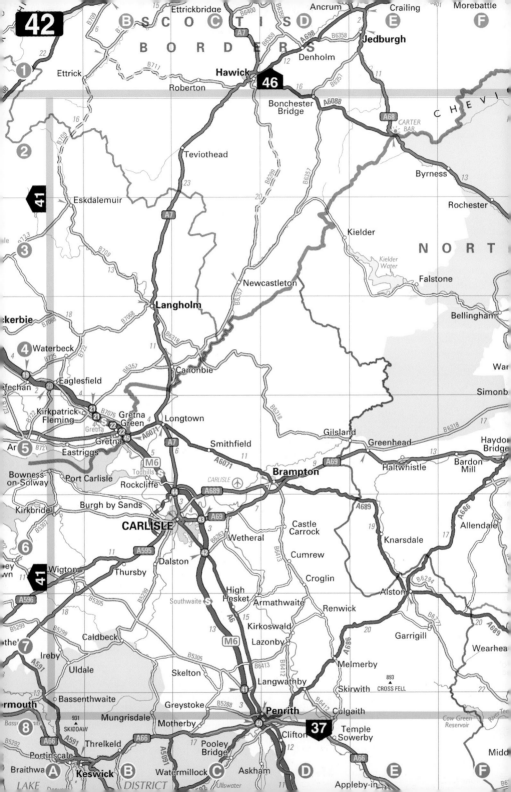

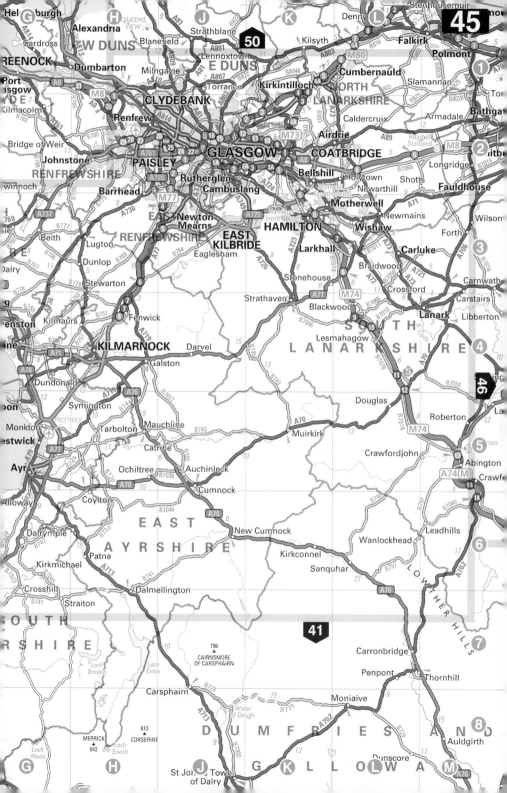

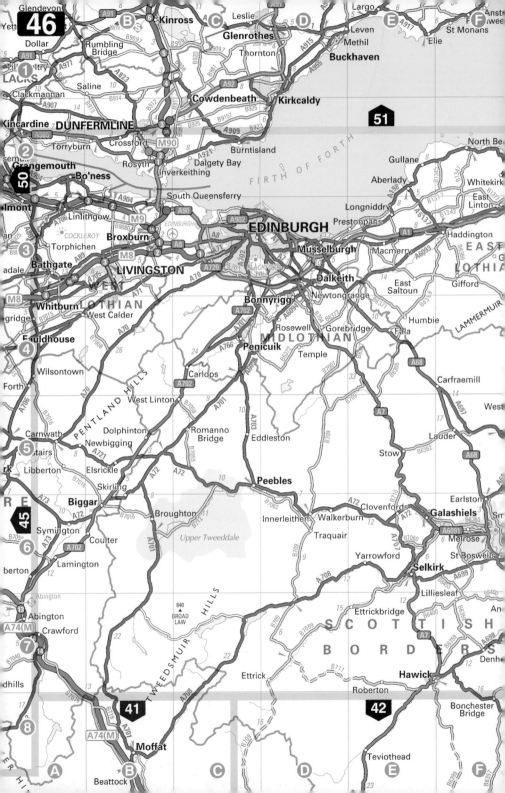

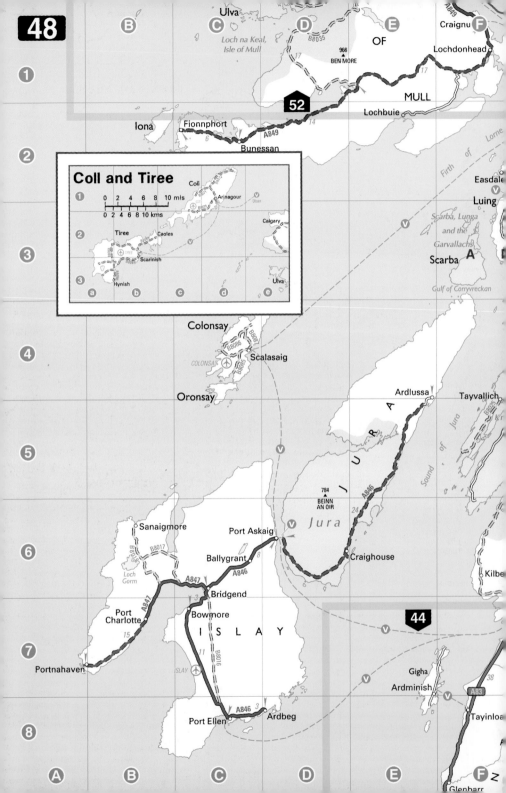

48

B C D E F

Ulva

Craignu

Loch na Keal,
Isle of Mull

1

OF

Lochdonhead

B8035

966
BEN MORE

52

17

MULL

Lochbuie

Iona Fionnphort

14

A849

Firth

Easdale

Bunessan

of

Luing

2

Lorne

Coll and Tiree

Coll

Scarba, Lunga
and the
Garvallachs

1

0 2 4 6 8 10 mls

Arinagour

A

0 2 4 6 8 10 kms

Calgary

Scarba

2

Tiree Caoles

3

Scarinish

Gulf of Corryvreckan

3

Hynish

Ulva

a b c d e

Colonsay

B8086 B808

4

B8086

Scalasaig

COLONSAY

B8085

Ardlussa

Tayvallich

Oronsay

J U R A

B8025

5

V

Sound

of

Jura

784
BEINN
AN OIR

Jura

24

Sanaigmore

Port Askaig

V

6

B8017

Ballygrant

8

Craighouse

B8018

A846

Kilbe

Loch
Gorm

A847

Bridgend

3

44

Port
Charlotte

A847

Bowmore

V

7

15

I S L A Y

Gigha

11

B8016

Ardminish

V

A83

38

Portnaven

ISLAY

V

Tayinloa

A846 3

8

Port Ellen Ardbeg

A B C D E F Z

Glenbarr

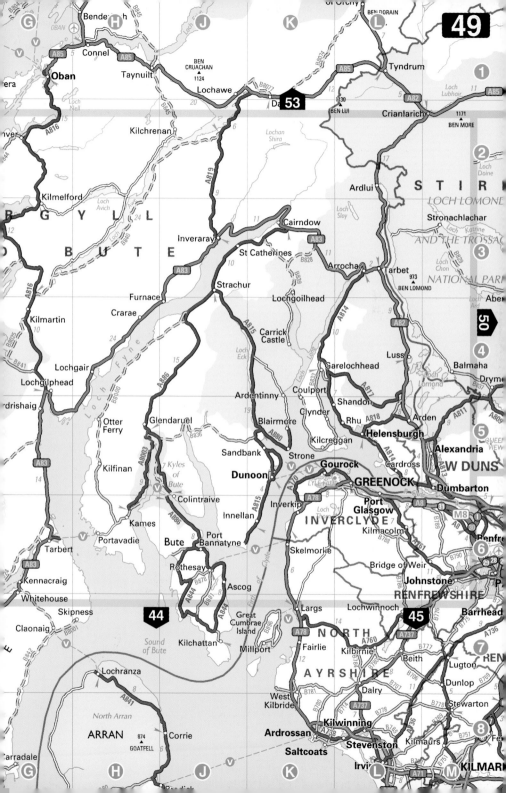

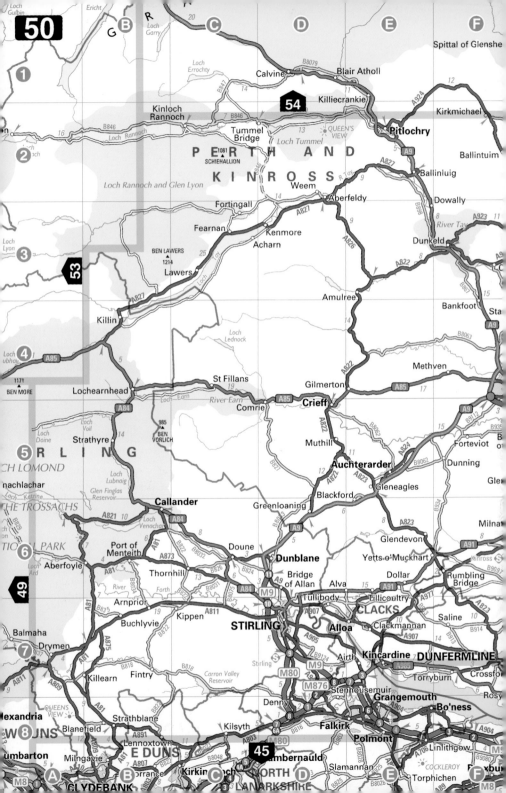

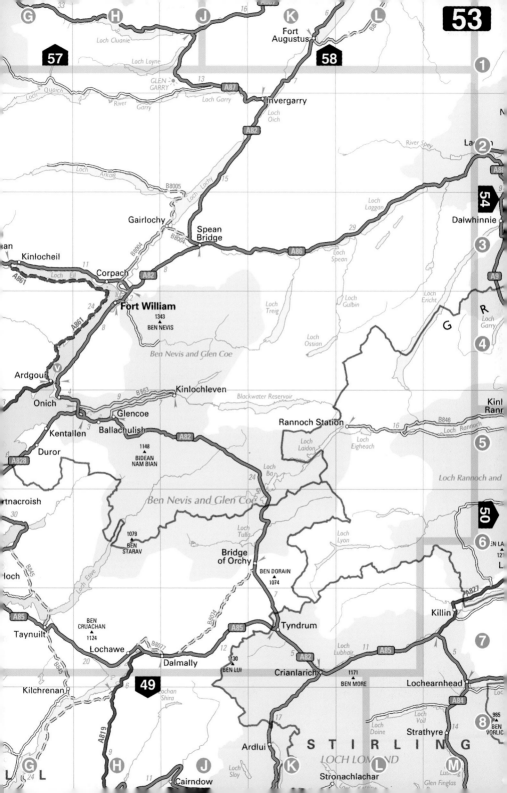

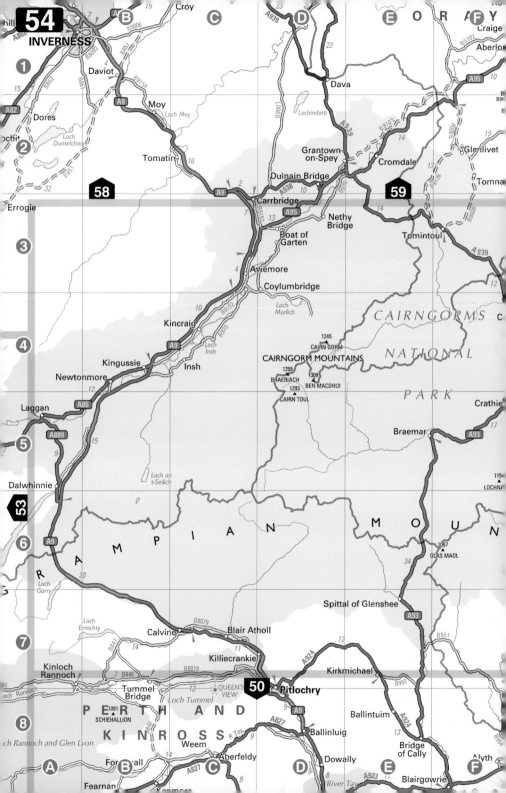

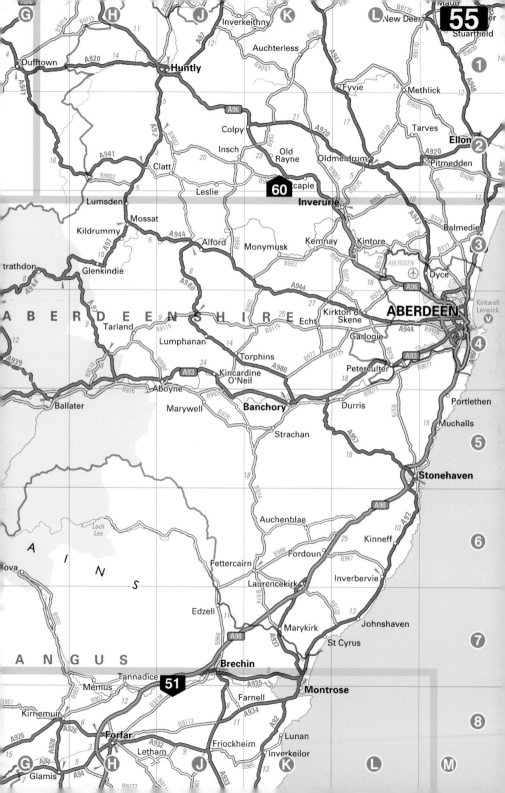

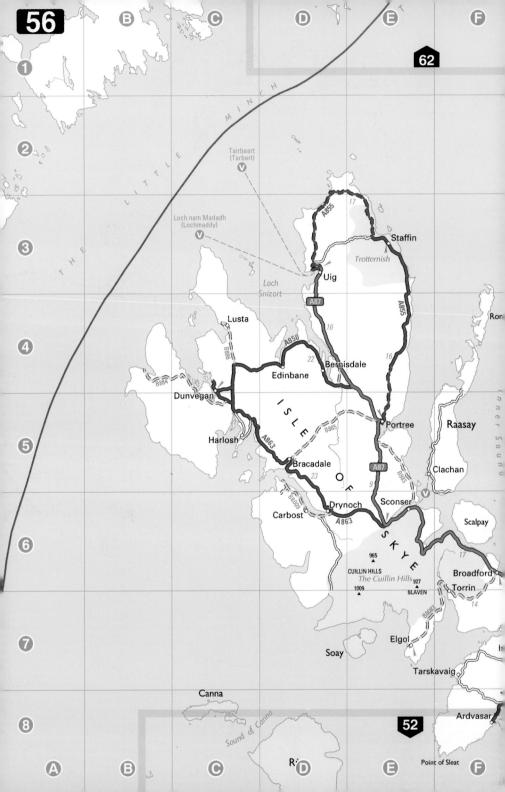

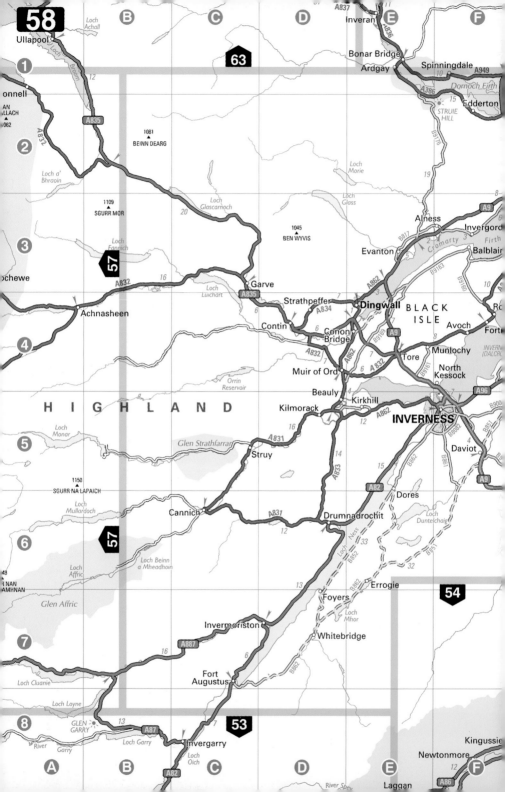

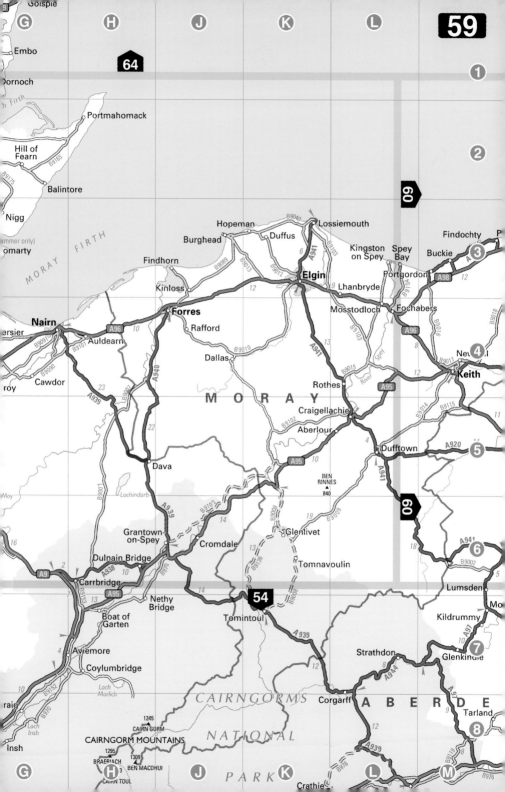

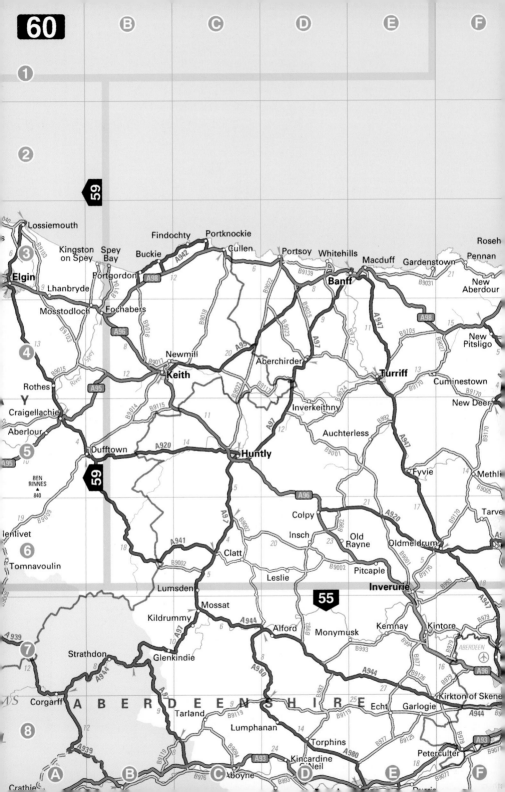

ndhaven

Fraserburgh

Inverallochy

St Combs

msie

Rathen

Crimond

strichen

St Fergus

Mintlaw

Deer

tfield

Longside

Clola

Boddam

Hatton

Cruden Bay

Collieston

Newburgh

Balmedie

ABERDEEN

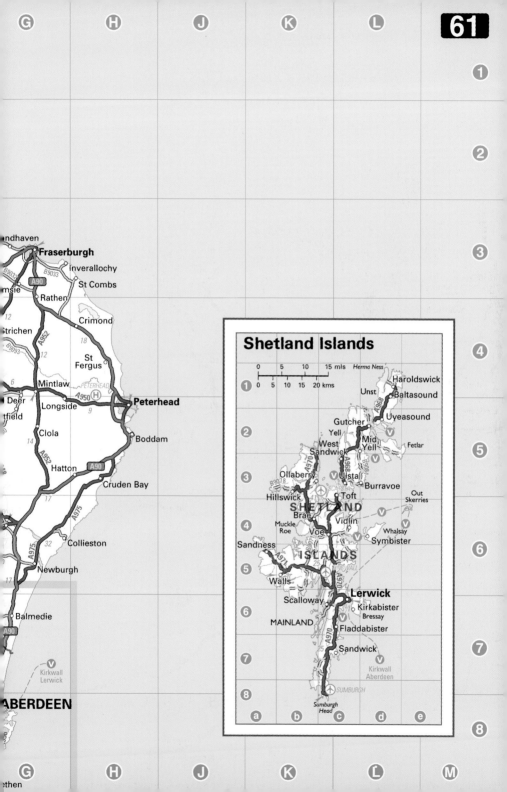

Shetland Islands

0   5   10   15 mls   *Herma Ness*

0   5   10   15   20 kms

Haroldswick

Unst   Baltasound

Uyeasound

Gutcher

Yell   Mid Yell

West Sandwick   Fetlar

Ollaberry   Ulsta

Hillswick   Toft   Burravoe   Out Skerries

SHETLAND

Brae

Muckle Roe   Vidlin

Voe   Whalsay

Sandness   Symbister

ISLANDS

Walls

Scalloway   **Lerwick**

Kirkabister

Bressay

MAINLAND   Fladdabister

Sandwick

Kirkwall Aberdeen

SUMBURGH

Sumburgh Head

ethen

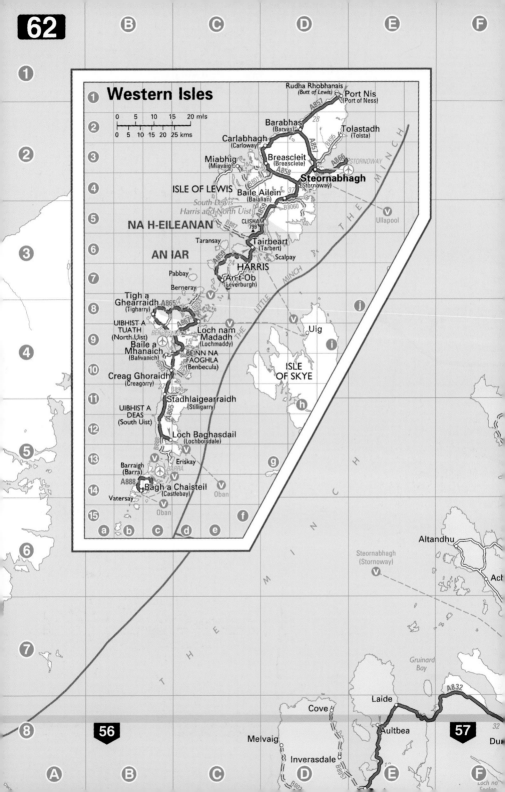

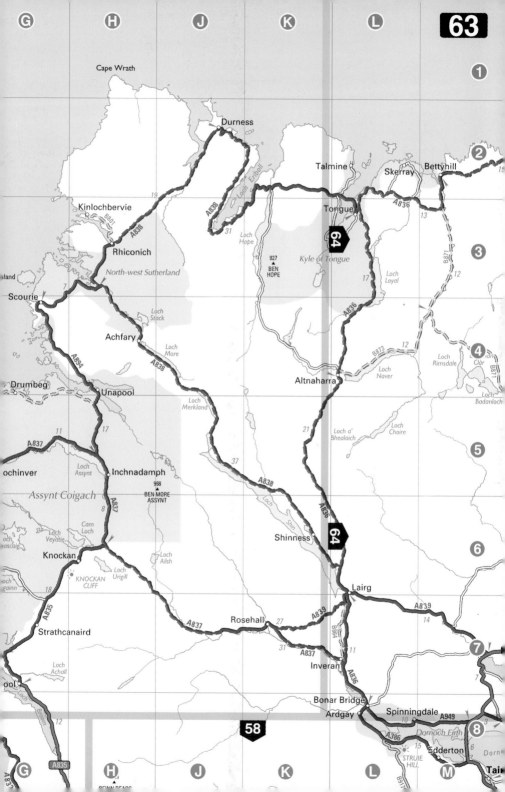

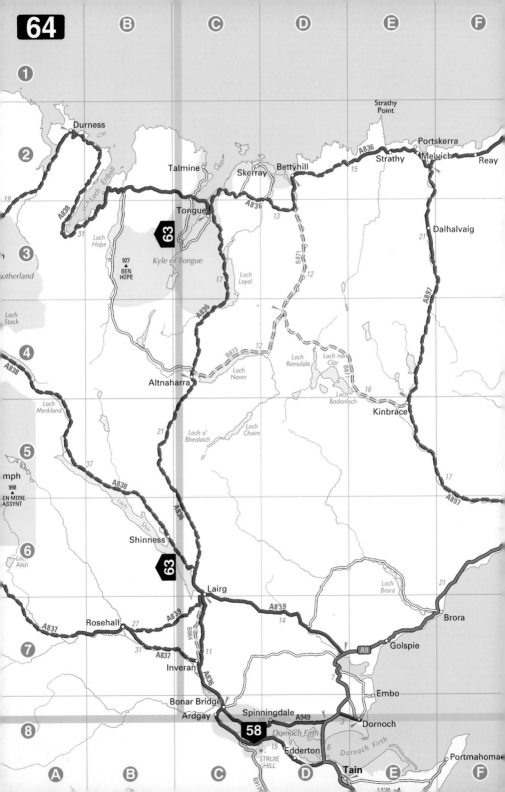

1

2

3

4

5

6

7

Stromness   V

Dunnet Head

Island of Stroma

St Margaret's Hope   V

crabster

Dunnet

Gills   A836   John o' Groats

Duncansby Head

15

B855

Thurso

Castletown

Freswick

5

B874

A9

Loch Calder

Halkirk

B876

B874

16

17   A99

Keiss

Loch hurrery

Spittal

B870

Watten   A882

B874

21

WICK

Wick

A9

23

Thrumster

Loch More

17   A99

Latheron

Lybster

Dunbeath

20

Berriedale

A9

nsdale

Orkney Islands

Mull Head

North Ronaldsay   1

Pierowall   Papa Westray

Westray   V

Midbea   Rapness

B9066

Sanday

Calfsound   Braeswick   2

Wasbister   Eday   Lerwick   V

Brough Head   Rousay   A966

O R K N E Y

Brinyan   Backaland

Downby   Hackland   Stronsay   3

MAINLAND   Finstown   Shapinsay   Balfour

A967   **Kirkwall**

Stromness   A964   V   4

Rora Head   Houton   A960   Aberdeen   V

HOY   Scapa Flow   St Mary's

Lyness   Flotta   Burray   St Margaret's Hope   5

V   A961   South Ronaldsay

Scrabster   Burwick

A961

V

0   5   10 mls

PENTLAND   FIRTH   0   5   10   15 kms   6

a   b   Gills   c   d

Index to places in Britain

This index lists places appearing in the main-map section of the atlas in alphabetical order. The reference before each name gives the atlas page number and grid reference of the square in which the place appears. The map shows counties, unitary authorities and administrative areas, together with a list of the abbreviated name forms used in the index.

England

BaNES	**Bath & N E Somerset (18)**
Barns	**Barnsley (19)**
Bed	**Bedford**
Birm	**Birmingham**
Bl w D	**Blackburn with Darwen (20)**
Bmouth	**Bournemouth**
Bolton	**Bolton (21)**
Bpool	**Blackpool**
Br & H	**Brighton & Hove (22)**
Br For	**Bracknell Forest (23)**
Bristl	**City of Bristol**
Bucks	**Buckinghamshire**
Bury	**Bury (24)**
C Beds	**Central Bedfordshire**
C Brad	**City of Bradford**
C Derb	**City of Derby**
C KuH	**City of Kingston upon Hull**
C Leic	**City of Leicester**
C Nott	**City of Nottingham**
C Pete	**City of Peterborough**
C Plym	**City of Plymouth**
C Port	**City of Portsmouth**
C Sotn	**City of Southampton**
C Stke	**City of Stoke-on-Trent**
C York	**City of York**
Calder	**Calderdale (25)**
Cambs	**Cambridgeshire**
Ches E	**Cheshire East**
Ches W	**Cheshire West and Chester**
Cnwll	**Cornwall**
Covtry	**Coventry**
Cumb	**Cumbria**
Darltn	**Darlington (26)**
Derbys	**Derbyshire**
Devon	**Devon**
Donc	**Doncaster (27)**
Dorset	**Dorset**
Dudley	**Dudley (28)**
Dur	**Durham**
E R Yk	**East Riding of Yorkshire**
E Susx	**East Sussex**
Essex	**Essex**
Gatesd	**Gateshead (29)**
Gloucs	**Gloucestershire**
Gt Lon	**Greater London**
Halton	**Halton (30)**
Hants	**Hampshire**
Hartpl	**Hartlepool (31)**
Herefs	**Herefordshire**
Herts	**Hertfordshire**
IoS	**Isles of Scilly**
IoW	**Isle of Wight**
Kent	**Kent**
Kirk	**Kirklees (32)**
Knows	**Knowsley (33)**
Lancs	**Lancashire**
Leeds	**Leeds**
Leics	**Leicestershire**
Lincs	**Lincolnshire**
Lpool	**Liverpool**
Luton	**Luton**
M Keyn	**Milton Keynes**
Manch	**Manchester**

Medway	**Medway**
Middsb	**Middlesbrough**
NE Lin	**North East Lincolnshire**
N Linc	**North Lincolnshire**
N Som	**North Somerset (34)**
N Tyne	**North Tyneside (35)**
N u Ty	**Newcastle upon Tyne**
N York	**North Yorkshire**
Nhants	**Northamptonshire**
Norfk	**Norfolk**
Notts	**Nottinghamshire**
Nthumb	**Northumberland**
Oldham	**Oldham (36)**
Oxon	**Oxfordshire**
Poole	**Poole**
R & Cl	**Redcar & Cleveland**
Readg	**Reading**
Rochdl	**Rochdale (37)**
Rothm	**Rotherham (38)**
Rutlnd	**Rutland**
S Glos	**South Gloucestershire (39)**
S on T	**Stockton-on-Tees (40)**
S Tyne	**South Tyneside (41)**
Salfd	**Salford (42)**
Sandw	**Sandwell (43)**
Sefton	**Sefton (44)**
Sheff	**Sheffield**
Shrops	**Shropshire**
Slough	**Slough (45)**
Solhll	**Solihull (46)**
Somset	**Somerset**
St Hel	**St Helens (47)**
Staffs	**Staffordshire**
Sthend	**Southend-on-Sea**
Stockp	**Stockport (48)**
Suffk	**Suffolk**
Sundld	**Sunderland**
Surrey	**Surrey**
Swindn	**Swindon**
Tamesd	**Tameside (49)**
Thurr	**Thurrock (50)**
Torbay	**Torbay**
Traffd	**Trafford (51)**
W & M	**Windsor and Maidenhead (52)**
W Berk	**West Berkshire**
W Susx	**West Sussex**
Wakefd	**Wakefield (53)**
Warrtn	**Warrington (54)**
Warwks	**Warwickshire**
Wigan	**Wigan (55)**
Wilts	**Wiltshire**
Wirral	**Wirral (56)**
Wokham	**Wokingham (57)**
Wolves	**Wolverhampton (58)**
Worcs	**Worcestershire**
Wrekin	**Telford & Wrekin (59)**
Wsall	**Walsall (60)**

Channel Islands & Isle of Man

Guern	**Guernsey**
Jersey	**Jersey**
IoM	**Isle of Man**

Scotland

Abers	**Aberdeenshire**
Ag & B	**Argyll and Bute**
Angus	**Angus**
Border	**Scottish Borders**
C Aber	**City of Aberdeen**
C Dund	**City of Dundee**
C Edin	**City of Edinburgh**
C Glas	**City of Glasgow**
Clacks	**Clackmannanshire (1)**
D & G	**Dumfries & Galloway**
E Ayrs	**East Ayrshire**
E Duns	**East Dunbartonshire (2)**
E Loth	**East Lothian**
E Rens	**East Renfrewshire (3)**
Falk	**Falkirk**
Fife	**Fife**
Highld	**Highland**
Inver	**Inverclyde (4)**
Mdloth	**Midlothian (5)**
Moray	**Moray**
N Ayrs	**North Ayrshire**
N Lans	**North Lanarkshire (6)**
Ork	**Orkney Islands**
P & K	**Perth & Kinross**
Rens	**Renfrewshire (7)**
S Ayrs	**South Ayrshire**
Shet	**Shetland Islands**
S Lans	**South Lanarkshire**
Stirlg	**Stirling**
W Duns	**West Dunbartonshire (8)**
W Isls	**Western Isles (Na h-Eileanan an Iar)**
W Loth	**West Lothian**

Wales

Blae G	**Blaenau Gwent (9)**
Brdgnd	**Bridgend (10)**
Caerph	**Caerphilly (11)**
Cardif	**Cardiff**
Carmth	**Carmarthenshire**
Cerdgn	**Ceredigion**
Conwy	**Conwy**
Denbgs	**Denbighshire**
Flints	**Flintshire**
Gwynd	**Gwynedd**
IoA	**Isle of Anglesey**
Mons	**Monmouthshire**
Myr Td	**Merthyr Tydfil (12)**
Neath	**Neath Port Talbot (13)**
Newpt	**Newport (14)**
Pembks	**Pembrokeshire**
Powys	**Powys**
Rhondd	**Rhondda Cynon Taff (15)**
Swans	**Swansea**
Torfn	**Torfaen (16)**
V Glam	**Vale of Glamorgan (17)**
Wrexhm	**Wrexham**

ORKNEY ISLANDS

SHETLAND ISLANDS

WESTERN ISLES (Na h-Eileanan an Iar)

HIGHLAND

MORAY

S C O T L A N D

ABERDEENSHIRE

Aberdeen

ANGUS

PERTH & KINROSS

Dundee

ARGYLL & BUTE

STIRLING

FIFE

1

8 FALK Edinburgh
2 E LOTH
Glasgow 6 W LOTH
7 3 5
NORTH AYRSHIRE
S LANS SCOTTISH BORDERS
E AYRS

S AYRS

DUMFRIES & GALLOWAY

NORTHUMBERLAND

Newcastle upon Tyne 35
29 41
Sunderland

DURHAM 31
CUMBRIA 26 40 R & CL
Middlesbrough

IoM

NORTH YORKSHIRE

Blackpool LANCASHIRE Bradford York EAST RIDING OF YORKSHIRE
Leeds Kingston upon Hull
20 25 53 N LINCS
21 24 37 32 19 27 N E LINCS
44 55 47 42 36 39
33 47 51 Manchester 38
Liverpool 54 30 48 Sheffield
56
IoA
CONWY FLINTS CHES E DERBYS
DENBGS W NOTTS LINCOLNSHIRE
WREXHAM Stoke-on- Nottingham
GWYNEDD Trent Derby
STAFFS NORFOLK
LEICS RUTLAND
59 Peterborough
SHROPSHIRE 68 60 Leicester
POWYS 28 43 Birmingham CAMBS
46 Coventry NHANTS
CERDGN WORCS WARWKS Milton SUFFOLK
Keynes BED
W A L E S HEREFS E N G L A N D BEDS Luton
PEMBKS HERTS ESSEX
CARMTH MONS GLOUCS OXON
9 BUCKS Southend-
13 12 16 GREATER on-Sea
Swansea 15 11 14 Reading 52 45 LONDON 50
10 Cardiff 39 Swindon 57 23 MEDWAY
17 Bristol W BERKS SURREY KENT
34 18 WILTSHIRE
SOMERSET HAMPSHIRE W SUSX E SUSX
DORSET Southampton 22
DEVON Bournemouth Portsmouth
Poole IoW
CORNWALL CHANNEL Guernsey
Plymouth Torbay ISLANDS
Jersey

IoS

Mileage chart - Britain

The mileage chart shows distances in miles between two towns along AA-recommended routes. Using motorways and other main roads this is normally the fastest route, though not necessarily the shortest.

Lincoln - Sheffield = 47 miles

1 mile = 1.6 kilometre

	Aberdeen	Aberystwyth	Barnstaple	Birmingham	Brighton	Bristol	Cambridge	Cardiff	Carlisle	Carmarthen	Dorchester	Dover	Edinburgh	Exeter	Fort William	Glasgow	Gloucester	Guildford	Holyhead	Hull	Inverness	Kendal	Leeds	Lincoln	Liverpool	Maidstone	Manchester	Middlesbrough	Newcastle	Norwich	Nottingham	Oxford	Penzance	Perth	Plymouth	Sheffield	Southampton	Stranraer	Taunton	Wick	York
Aberystwyth	472																																								
Barnstaple	608	214																																							
Birmingham	436	124	180																																						
Brighton	613	288	210	171																																					
Bristol	518	130	100	90	169																																				
Cambridge	463	215	267	97	120	170																																			
Cardiff	537	111	128	109	202	44	203																																		
Carlisle	236	236	371	199	376	281	256	300																																	
Carmarthen	520	48	190	172	264	107	266	68	284																																
Dorchester	600	206	94	172	119	62	184	120	364	182																															
Dover	587	326	272	208	82	205	124	239	381	301	200																														
Edinburgh	126	336	471	299	476	381	333	400	100	386	463	458																													
Exeter	593	198	44	165	178	84	259	113	356	175	57	248	455																												
Fort William	156	435	570	398	576	480	456	499	199	485	562	580	137	554																											
Glasgow	150	332	467	295	472	377	353	396	96	382	459	477	47	451	102																										
Gloucester	484	113	126	56	155	36	150	63	248	125	118	192	346	110	445	343																									
Guildford	571	224	175	128	44	106	96	139	335	201	97	97	433	150	532	430	99																								
Holyhead	464	102	339	167	345	249	259	202	228	150	331	369	326	323	425	323	215	302																							
Hull	376	227	320	139	258	230	138	250	170	311	312	262	247	304	367	266	196	239	218																						
Inverness	106	496	631	459	637	541	517	561	260	546	623	641	157	616	66	176	507	595	488	430																					
Kendal	283	189	324	153	330	234	251	254	47	240	316	354	145	309	245	143	200	288	181	164	307																				
Leeds	329	173	301	120	262	211	146	230	123	224	293	271	200	285	321	219	177	220	165	59	383	110																			
Lincoln	388	199	275	98	216	185	95	205	182	267	246	220	258	260	379	277	151	173	204	44	441	176	74																		
Liverpool	362	110	272	101	278	182	193	202	126	158	264	302	224	257	324	222	148	236	102	128	386	79	74	139																	
Maidstone	545	284	234	166	50	167	82	200	339	262	161	41	416	209	537	435	153	58	327	220	599	313	231	178	261																
Manchester	357	134	261	89	266	171	160	190	120	184	253	290	219	245	318	216	136	224	125	97	380	74	44	85	34	248															
Middlesbrough	276	244	357	176	318	267	197	286	95	294	349	322	146	341	283	190	232	276	235	89	308	84	64	122	145	280	114														
Newcastle	235	275	388	207	349	298	229	317	60	325	380	353	106	372	242	153	264	307	266	142	267	102	95	154	176	311	145	39													
Norwich	488	278	329	160	168	233	63	266	282	328	241	172	359	313	480	378	212	160	321	147	542	276	174	103	240	130	185	223	254												
Nottingham	395	162	232	51	193	142	86	161	189	223	224	210	266	216	387	285	107	151	178	93	449	164	77	39	112	168	71	130	161	119											
Oxford	510	160	170	68	109	73	82	107	274	169	115	146	373	154	472	370	48	67	242	190	534	228	174	132	176	107	164	227	258	146	102										
Penzance	702	308	108	274	287	193	368	222	466	284	167	357	564	109	663	562	220	259	434	415	726	419	403	370	367	318	356	451	482	433	326	265									
Perth	86	388	523	351	529	433	378	453	152	438	515	503	42	507	102	64	399	486	379	291	114	199	245	303	278	461	275	192	150	404	310	426	617								
Plymouth	633	239	62	205	218	124	299	153	397	215	98	288	495	44	594	493	151	190	365	346	657	350	334	301	298	249	287	382	413	364	257	196	78	544							
Sheffield	397	166	272	91	233	182	122	201	161	263	264	247	236	256	359	257	148	191	157	66	421	115	38	47	79	205	39	100	131	148	45	142	366	309	297						
Southampton	578	225	142	135	66	106	136	140	342	201	53	152	440	111	539	437	100	49	309	258	601	295	241	199	243	113	232	294	325	204	169	67	221	489	152	209					
Stranraer	235	342	477	305	482	387	363	406	106	392	469	487	132	461	181	86	352	440	333	276	261	153	229	288	232	445	229	201	163	388	295	380	571	149	502	267	447				
Taunton	560	165	50	132	160	51	226	80	323	142	45	224	422	34	521	419	77	126	291	272	583	277	261	228	225	185	213	309	340	291	184	123	144	471	75	224	94	429			
Wick	207	597	732	560	738	642	618	662	361	647	724	742	258	716	166	277	608	695	588	531	104	408	484	543	487	700	484	409	367	644	550	635	826	215	757	523	702	362	684		
York	323	201	314	133	275	224	154	243	116	251	306	279	193	298	314	212	189	233	192	38	376	91	24	79	102	237	71	51	89	180	87	184	408	239	339	57	251	223	265	477	
LONDON	550	239	216	121	54	120	59	153	314	215	125	78	413	200	512	410	102	31	282	186	574	268	201	143	216	39	204	254	285	118	129	56	310	462	241	169	77	420	167	675	211

Abberley - Bethesda 69

A

21 L4 **Abberley** Worcs
41 L6 **Abbey Town** Cumb
29 H7 **Abbots Bromley** Staffs
19 H1 **Aberaeron** Cerdgn
19 H1 **Aberarth** Cerdgn
60 D4 **Aberchirder** Abers
12 B2 **Aberdare** Rhondd
26 B6 **Aberdaron** Gwynd
55 M4 **Aberdeen** C Aber
20 A2 **Aberdyfi** Gwynd
50 D2 **Aberfeldy** P & K
26 C3 **Aberffraw** IoA
50 B6 **Aberfoyle** Stirlg
21 G8 **Abergavenny** Mons
27 H3 **Abergele** Conwy
46 E2 **Aberlady** E Loth
59 L5 **Aberlour** Moray
20 F2 **Abermule** Powys
51 G5 **Abernethy** P & K
18 F2 **Aberporth** Cerdgn
26 C6 **Abersoch** Gwynd
12 D2 **Abersychan** Torfn
12 D2 **Abertillery** Blae G
20 A3 **Aberystwyth** Cerdgn
14 C4 **Abingdon** Oxon
45 M5 **Abington** S Lans
30 D7 **Ab Kettleby** Leics
55 J4 **Aboyne** Abers
16 D7 **Abridge** Essex
33 G4 **Accrington** Lancs
52 D4 **Acharacle** Highld
50 C3 **Acharn** P & K
63 H4 **Achfary** Highld
62 F6 **Achiltibuie** Highld
52 F6 **Achnacroish** Ag & B
57 L4 **Achnasheen** Highld
34 B5 **Ackworth Moor Top** Wakefd
25 K5 **Acle** Norfk
29 G7 **Acton Trussell** Staffs
33 J2 **Addingham** C Brad
34 C6 **Adwick Le Street** Donc
38 D4 **Ainderby Steeple** N York
45 L2 **Airdrie** N Lans
50 E7 **Airth** Falk
21 L1 **Albrighton** Shrops
28 C7 **Albrighton** Shrops
9 K2 **Albury** Surrey
22 B4 **Alcester** Warwks
23 M3 **Alconbury** Cambs
14 A6 **Aldbourne** Wilts
35 J3 **Aldbrough** E R Yk
17 M2 **Aldeburgh** Suffk
8 C3 **Alderbury** Wilts
28 F3 **Alderley Edge** Ches E
14 D7 **Aldermaston** W Berk
22 D5 **Alderminster** Warwks
9 H2 **Aldershot** Hants
28 B4 **Aldford** Ches W
17 G5 **Aldham** Essex
13 L1 **Aldsworth** Gloucs
49 M5 **Alexandria** W Duns
9 K3 **Alfold** Surrey
55 J3 **Alford** Abers
31 K3 **Alford** Lincs
29 L4 **Alfreton** Derbys
10 D7 **Alfriston** E Susx
11 K4 **Alkham** Kent
47 H4 **Allanton** Border
42 F6 **Allendale** Nthumb
42 F7 **Allenheads** Nthumb
21 J6 **Allensmore** Herefs
50 E7 **Alloa** Clacks
41 L7 **Allonby** Cumb
45 G6 **Alloway** S Ayrs
13 G3 **Almondsbury** S Glos
58 F3 **Alness** Highld
43 K2 **Alnmouth** Nthumb
47 L7 **Alnwick** Nthumb
29 J7 **Alrewas** Staffs
28 E4 **Alsager** Ches E
42 E6 **Alston** Cumb
62 F6 **Altandhu** Highld
34 E5 **Althorpe** N Linc
64 C4 **Altnaharra** Highld
9 G2 **Alton** Hants
7 K2 **Alton Pancras** Dorset
28 E2 **Altrincham** Traffd
50 E6 **Alva** Clacks
13 G3 **Alveston** S Glos
51 G3 **Alyth** P & K
9 K4 **Amberley** W Susx
43 K2 **Amble** Nthumb
37 G3 **Ambleside** Cumb
15 G4 **Amersham** Bucks
8 C2 **Amesbury** Wilts
26 D1 **Amlwch** IoA
19 J5 **Ammanford** Carmth
38 F5 **Ampleforth** N York
23 K6 **Ampthill** C Beds
18 E5 **Amroth** Pembks
50 E3 **Amulree** P & K
30 F5 **Ancaster** Lincs
47 K5 **Ancroft** Nthumb
47 G7 **Ancrum** Border
8 D2 **Andover** Hants
22 B7 **Andoversford** Gloucs
36 c1 **Andreas** IoM
18 C6 **Angle** Pembks
9 K5 **Angmering** W Susx
41 M5 **Annan** D & G
43 J6 **Annfield Plain** Dur
30 C8 **Anstey** Leics
51 K6 **Anstruther** Fife
62 e7 **An t-Ob** W Isls
31 G5 **Anwick** Lincs
37 J2 **Appleby-in-Westmorland** Cumb
57 G5 **Applecross** Highld
4 D4 **Appledore** Devon
11 H5 **Appledore** Kent
38 A7 **Appletreewick** N York
51 L3 **Arbroath** Angus
28 C3 **Arclid Green** Ches E
48 D8 **Ardbeg** Ag & B
49 L5 **Arden** Ag & B
49 K4 **Ardentinny** Ag & B
59 G4 **Ardersier** Highld
64 C8 **Ardgay** Highld
53 G4 **Ardgour** Highld
10 C5 **Ardingly** W Susx
17 H4 **Ardleigh** Essex
49 L2 **Ardlui** Ag & B
48 E4 **Ardlussa** Ag & B
44 A3 **Ardminish** Ag & B
49 G5 **Ardrishaig** Ag & B
44 F4 **Ardrossan** N Ayrs
52 D1 **Ardvasar** Highld
40 C7 **Ardwell** D & G
48 d1 **Arinagour** Ag & B
52 D3 **Arisaig** Highld
37 J6 **Arkholme** Lancs
45 M2 **Armadale** W Loth
42 C7 **Armathwaite** Cumb
37 M6 **Arncliffe** N York
50 B7 **Arnprior** Stirlg
37 H5 **Arnside** Cumb
16 B3 **Arrington** Cambs
49 L3 **Arrochar** Ag & B
9 K5 **Arundel** W Susx
49 J6 **Ascog** Ag & B
15 G6 **Ascot** W & M
11 K3 **Ash** Kent
29 J5 **Ashbourne** Derbys
6 B5 **Ashburton** Devon
14 A5 **Ashbury** Oxon
29 K7 **Ashby-de-la-Zouch** Leics
12 E7 **Ashcott** Somset
11 H4 **Ashford** Kent
43 K3 **Ashington** Nthumb
9 L4 **Ashington** W Susx
16 E2 **Ashley** Cambs
33 H6 **Ashton-under-Lyne** Tamesd
8 D5 **Ashurst** Hants
4 D7 **Ashwater** Devon
36 F5 **Askam in Furness** Cumb
34 C5 **Askern** Donc
37 H2 **Askham** Cumb
37 M4 **Askrigg** N York
41 L7 **Aspatria** Cumb
14 B4 **Aston** Oxon
14 F3 **Aston Clinton** Bucks
21 H3 **Aston on Clun** Shrops
14 E4 **Aston Rowant** Oxon
28 C8 **Atcham** Shrops
22 D1 **Atherstone** Warwks
32 F6 **Atherton** Wigan
25 H6 **Attleborough** Norfk
25 H4 **Attlebridge** Norfk
35 H2 **Atwick** E R Yk
55 K6 **Auchenblae** Abers
41 H6 **Auchencairn** D & G
45 J5 **Auchinleck** E Ayrs
50 E5 **Auchterarder** P & K
60 E5 **Auchterless** Abers
51 G5 **Auchtermuchty** Fife
28 D5 **Audlem** Ches E
28 E5 **Audley** Staffs
59 H4 **Auldearn** Highld
41 J3 **Auldgirth** D & G
57 H1 **Aultbea** Highld
37 K6 **Austwick** N York
13 L4 **Avebury** Wilts
13 J2 **Avening** Gloucs
6 A6 **Aveton Gifford** Devon
54 C3 **Aviemore** Highld
58 F4 **Avoch** Highld
12 F4 **Avonmouth** Bristl
30 B5 **Awsworth** Notts
12 E5 **Axbridge** Somset
6 F3 **Axminster** Devon
6 F3 **Axmouth** Devon
14 F3 **Aylesbury** Bucks
11 K3 **Aylesham** Kent
25 J3 **Aylsham** Norfk
22 F6 **Aynho** Nhants
45 G5 **Ayr** S Ayrs
38 A4 **Aysgarth** N York
47 J4 **Ayton** Border

B

65 d2 **Backaland** Ork
25 K3 **Bacton** Norfk
33 H4 **Bacup** Lancs
38 E5 **Bagby** N York
62 b14 **Bagh a Chaisteil** W Isls
27 K3 **Bagillt** Flints
19 K6 **Baglan** Neath
14 F7 **Bagshot** Surrey
62 g4 **Baile Ailein** W Isls
62 c10 **Baile a Mhanaich** W Isls
37 M4 **Bainbridge** N York
34 F2 **Bainton** E R Yk
29 J3 **Bakewell** Derbys
27 H6 **Bala** Gwynd
62 g4 **Balallan** W Isls
51 G4 **Balbeggie** P & K
58 F3 **Balblair** Highld
10 B5 **Balcombe** W Susx
38 D5 **Baldersby** N York
16 B4 **Baldock** Herts
65 c3 **Balfour** Ork
59 G2 **Balintore** Highld
62 c10 **Balivanich** W Isls
53 H5 **Ballachulish** Highld
40 B4 **Ballantrae** S Ayrs
36 b4 **Ballasalla** IoM
55 G5 **Ballater** Abers
36 c2 **Ballaugh** IoM
50 E2 **Ballinluig** P & K
50 F2 **Ballintuim** P & K
48 C6 **Ballygrant** Ag & B
41 G4 **Balmaclellan** D & G
49 M4 **Balmaha** Stirlg
55 M3 **Balmedie** Abers
22 D3 **Balsall Common** Solhll
16 E3 **Balsham** Cambs
61 d1 **Baltasound** Shet
32 E4 **Bamber Bridge** Lancs
47 L6 **Bamburgh** Nthumb
29 J2 **Bamford** Derbys
37 H2 **Bampton** Cumb
5 H5 **Bampton** Devon
14 A4 **Bampton** Oxon
22 E6 **Banbury** Oxon
55 K5 **Banchory** Abers
60 E3 **Banff** Abers
26 E3 **Bangor** Gwynd
28 B5 **Bangor-is-y-coed** Wrexhm
25 H6 **Banham** Norfk
50 F4 **Bankfoot** P & K
10 B3 **Banstead** Surrey
62 h2 **Barabhas** W Isls
37 J5 **Barbon** Cumb
31 G3 **Bardney** Lincs
42 F5 **Bardon Mill** Nthumb
36 F5 **Bardsea** Cumb
22 D4 **Barford** Warwks
12 C2 **Bargoed** Caerph
16 C8 **Barking** Gt Lon
30 F5 **Barkston** Lincs
16 C4 **Barkway** Herts
16 C4 **Barley** Herts
34 E2 **Barmby Moor** E R Yk
26 E7 **Barmouth** Gwynd
39 L7 **Barmston** E R Yk
38 A2 **Barnard Castle** Dur
30 D2 **Barnby Moor** Notts
15 J4 **Barnet** Gt Lon
35 G6 **Barnetby le Wold** N Linc
33 H3 **Barnoldswick** Lancs
33 M6 **Barnsley** Barns
13 L2 **Barnsley** Gloucs
4 E4 **Barnstaple** Devon
40 D3 **Barr** S Ayrs
43 G4 **Barrasford** Nthumb
45 H3 **Barrhead** E Rens
40 D4 **Barrhill** S Ayrs
33 H3 **Barrowford** Lancs
36 E6 **Barrow-in-Furness** Cumb
30 C7 **Barrow upon Soar** Leics
5 K1 **Barry** V Glam
16 C2 **Barton** Cambs
32 E3 **Barton** Lancs
38 C3 **Barton** N York
23 L7 **Barton-le-Clay** C Beds
23 J3 **Barton Seagrave** Nhants
29 J7 **Barton-under-Needwood** Staffs
35 G5 **Barton-upon-Humber** N Linc
62 h2 **Barvas** W Isls
22 E2 **Barwell** Leics
16 F7 **Basildon** Essex
9 G1 **Basingstoke** Hants
29 J3 **Baslow** Derbys
42 A8 **Bassenthwaite** Cumb
31 G7 **Baston** Lincs
13 H5 **Bath** BaNES
46 A3 **Bathgate** W Loth
33 L4 **Batley** Kirk
10 F6 **Battle** E Susx
31 H3 **Baumber** Lincs
25 H4 **Bawdeswell** Norfk
17 L4 **Bawdsey** Suffk
34 D7 **Bawtry** Donc
36 F6 **Baycliff** Cumb
28 C8 **Bayston Hill** Shrops
15 G5 **Beaconsfield** Bucks
47 L6 **Beadnell** Nthumb
4 E5 **Beaford** Devon
47 K5 **Beal** Nthumb
7 H2 **Beaminster** Dorset
9 L2 **Beare Green** Surrey
10 F3 **Bearsted** Kent
41 L2 **Beattock** D & G
8 E5 **Beaulieu** Hants
58 D5 **Beauly** Highld
26 E3 **Beaumaris** IoA
7 b2 **Beaumont** Jersey
4 D7 **Beaworthy** Devon
27 L2 **Bebington** Wirral
25 L6 **Beccles** Suffk
13 L4 **Beckhampton** Wilts
30 E4 **Beckingham** Lincs
13 H6 **Beckington** Somset
24 E7 **Beck Row** Suffk
38 C4 **Bedale** N York
26 E5 **Beddgelert** Gwynd
23 K5 **Bedford** Bed
43 K4 **Bedlington** Nthumb
22 E2 **Bedworth** Warwks
35 H2 **Beeford** E R Yk
29 J3 **Beeley** Derbys
6 F3 **Beer** Devon
6 B7 **Beesands** Devon
28 C4 **Beeston** Ches W
30 B6 **Beeston** Notts
41 J5 **Beeswing** D & G
37 H5 **Beetham** Cumb
25 G4 **Beetley** Norfk
20 F3 **Beguildy** Powys
45 G3 **Beith** N Ayrs
47 L6 **Belford** Nthumb
42 F4 **Bellingham** Nthumb
44 A5 **Bellochantuy** Ag & B
45 K2 **Bellshill** N Lans
29 K5 **Belper** Derbys
43 H4 **Belsay** Nthumb
34 E6 **Belton** N Linc
25 L5 **Belton** Norfk
9 G6 **Bembridge** IoW
39 L6 **Bempton** E R Yk
52 F6 **Benderloch** Ag & B
10 F5 **Benenden** Kent
26 D2 **Benllech** IoA
14 D5 **Benson** Oxon
9 H2 **Bentley** Hants
24 B6 **Benwick** Cambs
3 K4 **Bere Alston** Devon
3 K4 **Bere Ferrers** Devon
7 L3 **Bere Regis** Dorset
13 G2 **Berkeley** Gloucs
15 G3 **Berkhamsted** Herts
56 D4 **Bernisdale** Highld
65 G5 **Berriedale** Highld
20 F1 **Berriew** Powys
12 D6 **Berrow** Somset
13 K8 **Berwick St John** Wilts
47 K4 **Berwick-upon-Tweed** Nthumb
11 G4 **Bethersden** Kent
26 E3 **Bethesda** Gwynd

64 D2 **Bettyhill** Highld
27 G4 **Betws-y-Coed** Conwy
27 H3 **Betws-yn-Rhos** Conwy
20 D5 **Beulah** Powys
35 G3 **Beverley** E R Yk
21 L3 **Bewdley** Worcs
10 F7 **Bexhill** E Susx
13 L1 **Bibury** Gloucs
14 D2 **Bicester** Oxon
5 H6 **Bickleigh** Devon
11 G4 **Biddenden** Kent
12 E6 **Biddisham** Somset
28 F4 **Biddulph** Staffs
4 D5 **Bideford** Devon
22 C5 **Bidford-on-Avon** Warwks
3 M6 **Bigbury-on-Sea** Devon
46 B6 **Biggar** S Lans
10 C3 **Biggin Hill** Gt Lon
23 M5 **Biggleswade** C Beds
17 H3 **Bildeston** Suffk
16 E7 **Billericay** Essex
31 G6 **Billingborough** Lincs
38 E2 **Billingham** on T
31 H4 **Billinghay** Lincs
9 K3 **Billingshurst** W Susx
31 K3 **Bilsby** Lincs
30 C4 **Bilsthorpe** Notts
35 H7 **Binbrook** Lincs
14 F6 **Binfield** Br For
30 D5 **Bingham** Notts
33 K3 **Bingley** C Brad
22 A8 **Birdlip** Gloucs
32 C7 **Birkenhead** Wirral
22 B2 **Birmingham** Birm
30 C8 **Birstall** Leics
43 K6 **Birtley** Gatesd
38 C1 **Bishop Auckland** Dur
21 G2 **Bishop's Castle** Shrops
22 A7 **Bishop's Cleeve** Gloucs
21 K5 **Bishop's Frome** Herefs
12 C7 **Bishops Lydeard** Somset
16 D5 **Bishop's Stortford** Herts
6 C4 **Bishopsteignton** Devon
19 J7 **Bishopston** Swans
13 M3 **Bishopstone** Swindn
13 G5 **Bishop Sutton** BaNES
8 F4 **Bishop's Waltham** Hants
30 F6 **Bitchfield** Lincs
13 G4 **Bitton** S Glos
22 F1 **Blaby** Leics
28 E6 **Blackbrook** Staffs
32 F4 **Blackburn** Bl w D
50 E6 **Blackford** P & K
19 M7 **Blackmill** Brdgnd
32 C3 **Blackpool** Bpool
4 D6 **Black Torrington** Devon
8 F6 **Blackwater** IoW
44 C5 **Blackwaterfoot** N Ayrs
12 C2 **Blackwood** Caerph
45 L4 **Blackwood** S Lans
14 C3 **Bladon** Oxon
26 F5 **Blaenau Ffestiniog** Gwynd
12 D1 **Blaenavon** Torfn
19 L6 **Blaengarw** Brdgnd
18 F2 **Blaenporth** Cerdgn
12 F5 **Blagdon** N Som
54 C7 **Blair Atholl** P & K
51 G3 **Blairgowrie** P & K
49 K5 **Blairmore** Ag & B
13 G1 **Blakeney** Gloucs
23 G5 **Blakesley** Nhants
43 G6 **Blanchland** Nthumb
7 L2 **Blandford Forum** Dorset
50 B8 **Blanefield** Stirlg
34 D6 **Blaxton** Donc
43 J5 **Blaydon** Gatesd
12 F6 **Bleadney** Somset
12 E5 **Bleadon** N Som
11 J3 **Blean** Kent
20 F4 **Bleddfa** Powys
10 B3 **Bletchingley** Surrey
23 J6 **Bletchley** M Keyn
23 K4 **Bletsoe** Bed
14 C5 **Blewbury** Oxon
25 J3 **Blickling** Norfk
30 C4 **Blidworth** Notts
10 C4 **Blindley Heath** Surrey

3 G4 **Blisland** Cnwll
22 E6 **Bloxham** Oxon
38 B7 **Blubberhouses** N York
5 J3 **Blue Anchor** Somset
43 K4 **Blyth** Nthumb
34 E7 **Blyton** Lincs
54 D3 **Boat of Garten** Highld
61 H5 **Boddam** Abers
27 J3 **Bodfari** Denbgs
26 C6 **Bodfuan** Gwynd
10 F5 **Bodiam** E Susx
3 G4 **Bodmin** Cnwll
9 J6 **Bognor Regis** W Susx
29 G3 **Bollington** Ches E
10 B6 **Bolney** W Susx
29 L3 **Bolsover** Derbys
32 F6 **Bolton** Bolton
33 J2 **Bolton Abbey** N York
37 H6 **Bolton le Sands** Lancs
1 H3 **Bolventor** Cnwll
64 C8 **Bonar Bridge** Highld
42 D1 **Bonchester Bridge** Border
46 A2 **Bo'ness** Falk
46 D4 **Bonnyrigg** Mdloth
26 D4 **Bontnewydd** Gwynd
12 B4 **Bonvilston** V Glam
36 E3 **Boot** Cumb
36 E4 **Bootle** Cumb
32 C7 **Bootle** Sefton
6 b1 **Bordeaux** Guern
10 E6 **Boreham Street** E Susx
15 J4 **Borehamwood** Herts
38 D6 **Boroughbridge** N York
10 E3 **Borough Green** Kent
29 L6 **Borrowash** Derbys
20 A2 **Borth** Cerdgn
26 E6 **Borth-y-Gest** Gwynd
3 G2 **Boscastle** Cnwll
9 H5 **Bosham** W Susx
20 B6 **Bosherston** Pembks
31 J5 **Boston** Lincs
34 B3 **Boston Spa** Leeds
25 H7 **Botesdale** Suffk
41 M7 **Bothel** Cumb
30 E6 **Bottesford** Leics
10 D4 **Bough Beech** Kent
11 H3 **Boughton Street** Kent
47 M7 **Boulmer** Nthumb
31 G7 **Bourne** Lincs
8 B6 **Bournemouth** Bmouth
21 K2 **Bourton** Shrops
22 C7 **Bourton-on-the-Water** Gloucs
6 B4 **Bovey Tracey** Devon
37 M3 **Bowes** Dur
48 C7 **Bowmore** Ag & B
41 M5 **Bowness-on-Solway** Cumb
13 J4 **Box** Wilts
17 H4 **Boxford** Suffk
23 J4 **Bozeat** Nhants
56 D5 **Bracadale** Highld
23 G6 **Brackley** Nhants
14 F6 **Bracknell** Br For
33 K4 **Bradford** C Brad
13 J5 **Bradford-on-Avon** Wilts
8 F6 **Brading** IoW
29 J2 **Bradwell** Derbys
17 H6 **Bradwell-on-Sea** Essex
4 C6 **Bradworthy** Devon
61 b4 **Brae** Shet
54 E5 **Braemar** Abers
65 d2 **Braeswick** Ork
45 L3 **Braidwood** S Lans
29 J5 **Brailsford** Derbys
16 F5 **Braintree** Essex
36 F2 **Braithwaite** Cumb
8 F3 **Bramdean** Hants
25 K7 **Bramfield** Suffk
34 B3 **Bramham** Leeds
33 L3 **Bramhope** Leeds
14 D7 **Bramley** Hants
9 K2 **Bramley** Surrey
23 M3 **Brampton** Cambs
42 D5 **Brampton** Cumb
8 D4 **Bramshaw** Hants
24 E2 **Brancaster** Norfk
35 H3 **Brandesburton** E R Yk
43 J7 **Brandon** Dur
24 E6 **Brandon** Suffk
22 E3 **Brandon** Warwks
6 E3 **Branscombe** Devon
8 C6 **Bransgore** Hants
30 F3 **Branston** Lincs

36 D2 **Branthwaite** Cumb
29 J4 **Brassington** Derbys
10 D3 **Brasted** Kent
13 J6 **Bratton** Wilts
3 K2 **Bratton Clovelly** Devon
4 F4 **Bratton Fleming** Devon
16 C5 **Braughing** Herts
4 E4 **Braunton** Devon
4 F4 **Brayford** Devon
62 g3 **Breascleit** W Isls
62 g3 **Breaclete** W Isls
19 H4 **Brechfa** Carmth
55 J7 **Brechin** Angus
11 G6 **Brede** E Susx
21 K5 **Bredenbury** Herefs
22 A6 **Bredon** Worcs
21 K5 **Bredwardine** Herefs
5 G3 **Brendon** Devon
12 E6 **Brent Knoll** Somset
16 F7 **Brentwood** Essex
11 H5 **Brenzett** Kent
28 E4 **Brereton Green** Ches E
28 F8 **Brewood** Staffs
36 C1 **Bride** IoM
3 L2 **Bridestowe** Devon
11 J3 **Bridge** Kent
48 C6 **Bridgend** Ag & B
19 L7 **Bridgend** Brdgnd
50 D6 **Bridge of Allan** Stirlg
51 G2 **Bridge of Cally** P & K
51 G5 **Bridge of Earn** P & K
53 K6 **Bridge of Orchy** Ag & B
49 M6 **Bridge of Weir** Rens
21 L2 **Bridgnorth** Shrops
12 E7 **Bridgwater** Somset
39 L6 **Bridlington** E R Yk
7 H3 **Bridport** Dorset
33 H3 **Brierfield** Lancs
35 G6 **Brigg** N Linc
41 L8 **Brigham** Cumb
33 K4 **Brighouse** Calder
8 E7 **Brighstone** IoW
17 J5 **Brightlingsea** Essex
10 B7 **Brighton** Br & H
23 K2 **Brigstock** Nhants
22 E3 **Brinklow** Warwks
13 K3 **Brinkworth** Wilts
65 c3 **Brinyan** Ork
6 C6 **Brixham** Torbay
3 L5 **Brixton** Devon
23 H3 **Brixworth** Nhants
13 L3 **Broad Blunsdon** Swindn
13 K8 **Broad Chalke** Wilts
6 D3 **Broadclyst** Devon
56 F6 **Broadford** Highld
18 C5 **Broad Haven** Pembks
11 L2 **Broadstairs** Kent
22 C6 **Broadway** Worcs
7 G2 **Broadwindsor** Dorset
25 J7 **Brockdish** Norfk
8 D5 **Brockenhurst** Hants
17 J1 **Brockford Street** Suffk
21 M8 **Brockworth** Gloucs
44 D4 **Brodick** N Ayrs
25 H7 **Brome** Suffk
21 J3 **Bromfield** Shrops
23 K5 **Bromham** Bed
10 C2 **Bromley** Gt Lon
39 J5 **Brompton-by-Sawdon** N York
5 H4 **Brompton Regis** Somset
22 A3 **Bromsgrove** Worcs
21 K5 **Bromyard** Herefs
20 F6 **Bronllys** Powys
25 K6 **Brooke** Norfk
11 H5 **Brookland** Kent
15 J4 **Brookmans Park** Herts
43 K2 **Broomhill** Nthumb
64 F7 **Brora** Highld
21 K1 **Broseley** Shrops
34 B4 **Brotherton** N York
39 G2 **Brotton** R & Cl
38 C7 **Brough** Cumb
54 B6 **Broughton** Border
34 F6 **Broughton** N Linc
36 F5 **Broughton-in-Furness** Cumb

13 M2 **Broughton Poggs** Oxon
29 H8 **Brownhills** Wsall
46 B3 **Broxburn** W Loth
16 D5 **Broxted** Essex
25 K5 **Brundall** Norfk
13 G7 **Bruton** Somset
19 K5 **Brynamman** Carmth
20 A1 **Bryncrug** Gwynd
12 C1 **Brynmawr** Blae G
34 D3 **Bubwith** E R Yk
50 B7 **Buchlyvie** Stirlg
23 M4 **Buckden** Cambs
37 M5 **Buckden** N York
6 B5 **Buckfastleigh** Devon
51 H6 **Buckhaven** Fife
13 H8 **Buckhorn Weston** Dorset
60 B3 **Buckie** Moray
23 G6 **Buckingham** Bucks
16 C4 **Buckland** Herts
8 E5 **Bucklers Hard** Hants
27 L4 **Buckley** Flints
28 E2 **Bucklow Hill** Ches E
30 E7 **Buckminster** Leics
4 B6 **Bude** Cnwll
6 D4 **Budleigh Salterton** Devon
2 F5 **Bugle** Cnwll
20 E5 **Builth Wells** Powys
8 C2 **Bulford** Wilts
22 E2 **Bulkington** Warwks
16 E8 **Bulphan** Thurr
23 K2 **Bulwick** Nhants
48 C2 **Bunessan** Ag & B
25 K6 **Bungay** Suffk
30 C6 **Bunny** Notts
16 C4 **Buntingford** Herts
25 H6 **Bunwell** Norfk
13 M5 **Burbage** Wilts
17 G4 **Bures** Essex
13 M1 **Burford** Oxon
10 B6 **Burgess Hill** W Susx
42 B6 **Burgh by Sands** Cumb
25 L5 **Burgh Castle** Norfk
59 J3 **Burghead** Moray
14 D6 **Burghfield** W Berk
31 K4 **Burgh le Marsh** Lincs
8 C5 **Burley** Hants
28 D5 **Burleydam** Ches E
33 K3 **Burley in Wharfedale** C Brad
28 C7 **Burlton** Shrops
38 C5 **Burneston** N York
24 F2 **Burnham Market** Norfk
17 H7 **Burnham-on-Crouch** Essex
12 D6 **Burnham-on-Sea** Somset
24 F2 **Burnham Overy Staithe** Norfk
33 G4 **Burnley** Lancs
43 J6 **Burnopfield** Dur
46 C2 **Burntisland** Fife
61 d3 **Burravoe** Shet
51 G3 **Burrelton** P & K
4 F5 **Burrington** Devon
19 H6 **Burry Port** Carmth
32 D5 **Burscough Bridge** Lancs
8 E5 **Bursledon** Hants
27 L3 **Burton** Ches W
39 K6 **Burton Agnes** E R Yk
7 H3 **Burton Bradstock** Dorset
39 K6 **Burton Fleming** E R Yk
37 H5 **Burton-in-Kendal** Cumb
30 C5 **Burton Joyce** Notts
23 J3 **Burton Latimer** Nhants
34 F5 **Burton upon Stather** N Linc
29 J7 **Burton upon Trent** Staffs
10 E5 **Burwash** E Susx
24 E1 **Burwell** Cambs
65 c6 **Burwick** Ork
33 G5 **Bury** Bury
17 G2 **Bury St Edmunds** Suffk
15 H4 **Bushey** Herts
17 L8 **Butley** Suffk
36 E2 **Buttermere** Cumb
31 J5 **Butterwick** Lincs
27 K8 **Buttington** Powys
10 D6 **Buxted** E Susx

29 H3 **Buxton** Derbys
20 F7 **Bwlch** Powys
15 H7 **Byfleet** Surrey
27 H4 **Bylchau** Conwy
42 F2 **Byrness** Nthumb

C

2 D8 **Cadgwith** Cnwll
12 E3 **Caerleon** Newpt
26 D4 **Caernarfon** Gwynd
12 C3 **Caerphilly** Caerph
20 E2 **Caersws** Powys
12 F3 **Caerwent** Mons
27 J3 **Caerwys** Flints
49 K3 **Cairndow** Ag & B
40 B5 **Cairnryan** D & G
25 L5 **Caister-on-Sea** Norfk
35 H6 **Caistor** Lincs
42 B7 **Caldbeck** Cumb
23 J2 **Caldecott** Rutlnd
36 D3 **Calder Bridge** Cumb
45 L2 **Caldercruix** N Lans
12 F3 **Caldicot** Mons
65 d2 **Calfsound** Ork
52 B5 **Calgary** Ag & B
50 B6 **Callander** Stirlg
3 J4 **Callington** Cnwll
13 K4 **Calne** Wilts
8 E5 **Calshot** Hants
54 C7 **Calvine** P & K
11 H6 **Camber** E Susx
14 F7 **Camberley** Surrey
43 H4 **Cambo** Nthumb
2 C6 **Camborne** Cnwll
16 B2 **Cambourne** Cambs
16 C2 **Cambridge** Cambs
13 H2 **Cambridge** Gloucs
45 K2 **Cambuslang** S Lans
15 K5 **Camden Town** Gt Lon
3 G3 **Camelford** Cnwll
44 B5 **Campbeltown** Ag & B
31 K3 **Candlesby** Lincs
58 C6 **Cannich** Highld
12 D7 **Cannington** Somset
29 G8 **Cannock** Staffs
42 C4 **Canonbie** D & G
11 J3 **Canterbury** Kent
16 F8 **Canvey Island** Essex
48 D2 **Caoles** Ag & B
9 L2 **Capel** Surrey
20 B3 **Capel Bangor** Cerdgn
26 F4 **Capel Curig** Conwy
17 J4 **Capel St Mary** Suffk
50 F3 **Caputh** P & K
56 D6 **Carbost** Highld
12 C4 **Cardiff** Cardif
18 E2 **Cardigan** Cerdgn
23 L5 **Cardington** Bed
49 L5 **Cardross** Ag & B
18 D6 **Carew** Pembks
46 F4 **Carfraemill** Border
5 J3 **Carhampton** Somset
37 G5 **Cark** Cumb
62 g3 **Carlabhagh** W Isls
42 C6 **Carlisle** Cumb
46 C4 **Carlops** Border
62 g3 **Carloway** W Isls
34 D4 **Carlton** N York
38 A5 **Carlton** N York
30 E4 **Carlton-on-Trent** Notts
45 L3 **Carluke** S Lans
19 G4 **Carmarthen** Carmth
39 K6 **Carnaby** E R Yk
37 H6 **Carnforth** Lancs
20 D2 **Carno** Powys
2 E6 **Carnon Downs** Cnwll
51 K4 **Carnoustie** Angus
46 A5 **Carnwath** S Lans
44 C4 **Carradale** Ag & B
59 H6 **Carrbridge** Highld
7 b1 **Carrefour** Jersey
49 K4 **Carrick Castle** Ag & B
41 J3 **Carronbridge** D & G
41 L5 **Carrutherstown** D & G
40 F3 **Carsphairn** D & G
45 M3 **Carstairs** S Lans
14 A3 **Carterton** Oxon
37 G5 **Cartmel** Cumb
6 a2 **Castel** Guern
37 J5 **Casterton** Cumb
24 F4 **Castle Acre** Norfk
62 b14 **Castlebay** W Isls
42 D6 **Castle Carrock** Cumb
13 G2 **Castle Cary** Somset
29 L6 **Castle Donington** Leics

41 H5 **Castle Douglas** D & G
34 B4 **Castleford** Wakefd
16 B4 **Castle Hedingham** Essex
18 C6 **Castlemartin** Pembks
24 D4 **Castle Rising** Norfk
43 H6 **Castleside** Dur
29 H2 **Castleton** Derbys
39 G3 **Castleton** N York
12 D3 **Castleton** Newpt
65 H2 **Castletown** Highld
36 b4 **Castletown** IoM
10 C3 **Caterham** Surrey
25 K4 **Catfield** Norfk
37 H6 **Caton** Lancs
45 J5 **Catrine** E Ayrs
10 F6 **Catsfield** E Susx
38 C4 **Catterick** N York
30 D4 **Caunton** Notts
59 G4 **Cawdor** Highld
3 K5 **Cawsand** Cnwll
16 B2 **Caxton** Cambs
30 F5 **Caythorpe** Lincs
39 K5 **Cayton** N York
26 C1 **Cemaes** IoA
20 C1 **Cemmaes Road** Powys
51 J5 **Ceres** Fife
7 J2 **Cerne Abbas** Dorset
27 H5 **Cerrigydrudion** Conwy
33 H6 **Chadderton** Oldham
14 B2 **Chadlington** Oxon
6 A3 **Chagford** Devon
8 E7 **Chale** IoW
15 G4 **Chalfont St Giles** Bucks
15 G5 **Chalfont St Peter** Bucks
13 J2 **Chalford** Gloucs
4 F3 **Challacombe** Devon
11 H3 **Challock** Kent
8 E4 **Chandler's Ford** Hants
29 H2 **Chapel-en-le-Frith** Derbys
31 L3 **Chapel St Leonards** Lincs
34 A6 **Chapeltown** Sheff
13 J6 **Chapmanslade** Wilts
6 F2 **Chard** Somset
11 H4 **Charing** Kent
14 B2 **Charlbury** Oxon
22 D5 **Charlecote** Warwks
22 A7 **Charlton Kings** Gloucs
7 L2 **Charlton Marshall** Dorset
10 B4 **Charlwood** Surrey
7 G3 **Charmouth** Dorset
11 J3 **Chartham** Kent
33 G3 **Chatburn** Lancs
10 F2 **Chatham** Medway
24 B7 **Chatteris** Cambs
47 K6 **Chatton** Nthumb
4 F6 **Chawleigh** Devon
9 G3 **Chawton** Hants
29 G5 **Cheadle** Staffs
33 H7 **Cheadle** Stockp
29 G5 **Cheddar** Somset
29 G5 **Cheddleton** Staffs
28 F3 **Chelford** Ches E
16 F6 **Chelmsford** Essex
22 A7 **Cheltenham** Gloucs
12 F3 **Chepstow** Mons
8 F3 **Cheriton** Hants
5 H6 **Cheriton Fitzpaine** Devon
15 G6 **Chertsey** Surrey
15 G6 **Chesham** Bucks
15 K4 **Cheshunt** Herts
28 B3 **Chester** Ches W
29 K3 **Chesterfield** Derbys
43 G4 **Chester-le-Street** Dur
13 G5 **Chew Magna** BaNES
13 G6 **Chewton Mendip** Somset
23 J5 **Chicheley** M Keyn
9 H5 **Chichester** W Susx
7 J4 **Chickerell** Dorset
13 J7 **Chicklade** Wilts
9 J3 **Chiddingfold** Surrey
14 C6 **Chieveley** W Berk
16 C7 **Chigwell** Essex
28 B3 **Childer Thornton** Ches W
11 J3 **Chilham** Kent
6 B7 **Chillington** Devon
13 K7 **Chilmark** Wilts
5 K7 **Chilsworthy** Devon
14 A6 **Chilton Foliat** Wilts
14 E4 **Chinnor** Oxon

16 E1 **Chippenham** Cambs
13 J4 **Chippenham** Wilts
15 G4 **Chipperfield** Herts
32 F3 **Chipping** Lancs
22 C6 **Chipping Campden** Gloucs
22 D7 **Chipping Norton** Oxon
16 D6 **Chipping Ongar** Essex
13 H3 **Chipping Sodbury** S Glos
22 F5 **Chipping Warden** Nhants
21 G1 **Chirbury** Shrops
27 L6 **Chirk** Wrexhm
47 J4 **Chirnside** Border
13 M4 **Chiseldon** Swindn
13 K6 **Chitterne** Wilts
4 F5 **Chittlehamholt** Devon
15 G7 **Chobham** Surrey
8 C2 **Cholderton** Wilts
32 E5 **Chorley** Lancs
15 G4 **Chorleywood** Herts
8 C6 **Christchurch** Dorset
6 C4 **Chudleigh** Devon
6 C4 **Chudleigh Knighton** Devon
4 F6 **Chulmleigh** Devon
14 A2 **Churchill** Oxon
21 G2 **Churchstoke** Powys
21 H2 **Church Stretton** Shrops
6 C6 **Churston Ferrers** Torbay
9 H3 **Churt** Surrey
21 K8 **Cinderford** Gloucs
13 K2 **Cirencester** Gloucs
44 B3 **Clachan** Ag & B
56 E5 **Clachan** Highld
50 E7 **Clackmannan** Clacks
17 J5 **Clacton-on-Sea** Essex
14 A4 **Clanfield** Oxon
44 C3 **Claonaig** Ag & B
23 K5 **Clapham** Bed
37 K6 **Clapham** N York
16 F3 **Clare** Suffk
60 C6 **Clatt** Abers
22 C4 **Claverdon** Warwks
16 D4 **Clavering** Essex
4 C7 **Clawton** Devon
29 K4 **Clay Cross** Derbys
17 J3 **Claydon** Suffk
36 D2 **Cleator Moor** Cumb
35 J6 **Cleethorpes** NE Lin
12 F5 **Cleeve** N Som
22 B7 **Cleeve Hill** Gloucs
21 K3 **Cleobury Mortimer** Shrops
21 K2 **Cleobury North** Shrops
12 E4 **Clevedon** N Som
32 C3 **Cleveleys** Lancs
25 G2 **Cley next the Sea** Norfk
10 F2 **Cliffe** Medway
34 D4 **Cliffe** N York
10 F2 **Cliffe Woods** Medway
37 H2 **Clifton** Cumb
21 L4 **Clifton upon Teme** Worcs
9 K5 **Climping** W Susx
33 G3 **Clitheroe** Lancs
61 G5 **Clola** Abers
23 L6 **Clophill** C Beds
7 H2 **Closworth** Somset
39 J4 **Cloughton** N York
55 G6 **Clova** Angus
4 C5 **Clovelly** Devon
46 E6 **Clovenfords** Border
30 B3 **Clowne** Derbys
21 L3 **Clows Top** Worcs
21 G3 **Clun** Shrops
19 J6 **Clydach** Swans
45 H2 **Clydebank** W Duns
49 K5 **Clynder** Ag & B
26 D5 **Clynnog-fawr** Gwynd
20 F6 **Clyro** Powys
6 D3 **Clyst St Mary** Devon
21 K1 **Coalport** Wrekin
29 L7 **Coalville** Leics
45 K2 **Coatbridge** N Lans
10 E2 **Cobham** Kent
47 H3 **Cockburnspath** Border
41 L8 **Cockermouth** Cumb
9 J4 **Cocking** W Susx
17 J2 **Coddenham** Suffk
13 K7 **Codford St Mary** Wilts
15 J3 **Codicote** Herts
29 L5 **Codnor** Derbys

21 M1 **Codsall** Staffs
27 L5 **Coedpoeth** Wrexhm
12 G5 **Coggeshall** Essex
17 H5 **Colchester** Essex
14 C6 **Cold Ash** W Berk
23 G3 **Cold Ashby** Nhants
13 H4 **Cold Ashton** S Glos
47 J3 **Coldingham** Border
17 G7 **Cold Norton** Essex
47 H5 **Coldstream** Border
13 G1 **Coleford** Gloucs
13 J4 **Colerne** Wilts
22 C2 **Coleshill** Warwks
49 J6 **Colintraive** Ag & B
15 K2 **Collier's End** Herts
61 G6 **Collieston** Abers
13 M6 **Collingbourne Ducis** Wilts
34 B3 **Collingham** Leeds
40 C3 **Colmonell** S Ayrs
33 H3 **Colne** Lancs
17 G4 **Colne Engaine** Essex
13 L2 **Coln St Aldwyns** Gloucs
60 D6 **Colpy** Abers
30 F7 **Colsterworth** Lincs
25 J4 **Coltishall** Norfk
43 G4 **Colwell** Nthumb
27 G2 **Colwyn Bay** Conwy
6 F3 **Colyford** Devon
6 F3 **Colyton** Devon
4 E3 **Combe Martin** Devon
9 J2 **Compton** Surrey
14 C5 **Compton** W Berk
50 D5 **Comrie** P & K
28 F4 **Congleton** Ches E
12 E5 **Congresbury** N Som
31 H4 **Coningsby** Lincs
23 M2 **Conington** Cambs
34 C6 **Conisbrough** Donc
36 F4 **Coniston** Cumb
27 L3 **Connah's Quay** Flints
52 F7 **Connel** Ag & B
58 E4 **Conon Bridge** Highld
43 H6 **Consett** Dur
2 D7 **Constantine** Cnwll
58 D4 **Contin** Highld
27 G3 **Conwy** Conwy
14 F5 **Cookham** W & M
9 L4 **Coolham** W Susx
8 B3 **Coombe Bissett** Wilts
21 M7 **Coombe Hill** Gloucs
17 J3 **Copdock** Suffk
17 G5 **Copford Green** Essex
38 B2 **Copley** Dur
5 G6 **Copplestone** Devon
10 B4 **Copthorne** W Susx
7 a2 **Corbiere** Jersey
43 G5 **Corbridge** Nthumb
23 J2 **Corby** Nhants
30 F7 **Corby Glen** Lincs
6 F1 **Corfe** Somset
7 M4 **Corfe Castle** Dorset
55 G4 **Corgarff** Abers
47 H5 **Cornhill-on-Tweed** Nthumb
3 L5 **Cornwood** Devon
53 H3 **Corpach** Highld
44 D4 **Corrie** N Ayrs
26 F8 **Corris** Gwynd
13 J4 **Corsham** Wilts
13 J3 **Corston** Wilts
25 M6 **Corton** Suffk
27 J5 **Corwen** Denbgs
16 F8 **Coryton** Thurr
22 F2 **Cosby** Leics
28 D4 **Cotebrook** Ches W
38 A2 **Cotherstone** Dur
16 C1 **Cottenham** Cambs
16 B4 **Cottered** Herts
35 G4 **Cottingham** E R Yk
49 K5 **Coulport** Ag & B
46 B6 **Coulter** S Lans
23 G2 **Countesthorpe** Leics
51 G3 **Coupar Angus** P & K
62 D8 **Cove** Highld
22 E3 **Coventry** Covtry
2 D8 **Coverack** Cnwll
31 H7 **Cowbit** Lincs
12 B4 **Cowbridge** V Glam
10 D4 **Cowden** Kent
51 G7 **Cowdenbeath** Fife
8 E6 **Cowes** IoW
9 L4 **Cowfold** W Susx
33 J3 **Cowling** N York
10 F3 **Coxheath** Kent
38 E5 **Coxwold** N York
44 H6 **Coylton** S Ayrs
54 D3 **Coylumbridge** Highld

4 B7 **Crackington Haven** Cnwll
37 M7 **Cracoe** N York
3 J5 **Crafthole** Cnwll
59 L5 **Craigellachie** Moray
48 D6 **Craighouse** Ag & B
52 E6 **Craignure** Ag & B
51 J5 **Craigrothie** Fife
51 L6 **Crail** Fife
47 G7 **Crailing** Border
43 K4 **Cramlington** Nthumb
8 B4 **Cranborne** Dorset
10 F5 **Cranbrook** Kent
23 K6 **Cranfield** C Beds
21 M8 **Cranham** Gloucs
9 K2 **Cranleigh** Surrey
47 G4 **Cranshaws** Border
49 H4 **Crarae** Ag & B
47 M7 **Craster** Nthumb
54 F5 **Crathie** Abers
38 E3 **Crathorne** N York
21 H3 **Craven Arms** Shrops
46 A7 **Crawford** S Lans
45 M5 **Crawfordjohn** S Lans
10 B5 **Crawley** W Susx
10 B4 **Crawley Down** W Susx
62 c10 **Creag Ghoraidh** W Isls
62 c10 **Creagorry** W Isls
21 H6 **Credenhill** Herefs
5 G7 **Crediton** Devon
40 F6 **Creetown** D & G
36 a4 **Cregneash** IoM
21 K1 **Cressage** Shrops
28 E4 **Crewe** Ches E
7 G2 **Crewkerne** Somset
53 K7 **Crianlarich** Stirlg
26 D6 **Criccieth** Gwynd
20 F7 **Crickhowell** Powys
13 L3 **Cricklade** Wilts
50 D5 **Crieff** P & K
61 H4 **Crimond** Abers
49 G4 **Crinan** Ag & B
25 J5 **Cringleford** Norfk
6 B3 **Crockernwell** Devon
41 J4 **Crocketford** D & G
42 D6 **Croglin** Cumb
59 G3 **Cromarty** Highld
59 J6 **Cromdale** Highld
25 J2 **Cromer** Norfk
29 K4 **Cromford** Derbys
30 E4 **Cromwell** Notts
43 J7 **Crook** Dur
37 H5 **Crooklands** Cumb
22 F5 **Cropredy** Oxon
39 G4 **Cropton** N York
36 b3 **Crosby** IoM
32 C6 **Crosby** Sefton
46 B2 **Crossford** Fife
45 L3 **Crossford** S Lans
19 H5 **Cross Hands** Carmth
45 G6 **Crosshill** S Ayrs
10 D6 **Cross in Hand** E Susx
12 D3 **Crosskeys** Caerph
41 H5 **Crossmichael** D & G
21 M4 **Crossway Green** Worcs
37 G4 **Crosthwaite** Cumb
10 D5 **Crowborough** E Susx
5 K4 **Crowcombe** Somset
10 F6 **Crowhurst** E Susx
31 H8 **Crowland** Lincs
34 E5 **Crowle** N Linc
14 F7 **Crowthorne** Wokham
30 E6 **Croxton Kerrial** Leics
59 G4 **Croy** Highld
4 D4 **Croyde** Devon
15 K7 **Croydon** Gt Lon
61 H5 **Cruden Bay** Abers
28 D7 **Crudgington** Wrekin
13 K3 **Crudwell** Wilts
19 K5 **Crynant** Neath
10 B5 **Cuckfield** W Susx
30 C3 **Cuckney** Notts
28 D3 **Cuddington** Ches W
34 B6 **Cudworth** Barns
15 K4 **Cuffley** Herts
37 J1 **Culgaith** Cumb
60 C3 **Cullen** Moray
5 J6 **Cullompton** Devon
5 K6 **Culmstock** Devon
45 L1 **Cumbernauld** N Lans
60 E4 **Cuminestown** Abers
41 L5 **Cummertrees** D & G
45 J5 **Cumnock** E Ayrs
14 C4 **Cumnor** Oxon
42 D6 **Cumrew** Cumb
51 J5 **Cupar** Fife

D

40 D2 **Dailly** S Ayrs
51 J5 **Dairsie** Fife
41 J5 **Dalbeattie** D & G
36 a3 **Dalby** IoM
18 B5 **Dale** Pembks
46 C2 **Dalgety Bay** Fife
64 E3 **Dalhalvaig** Highld
46 D3 **Dalkeith** Mdloth
59 J4 **Dallas** Moray
53 J7 **Dalmally** Ag & B
45 H7 **Dalmellington** E Ayrs
45 G3 **Dalry** N Ayrs
45 G6 **Dalrymple** E Ayrs
42 B6 **Dalston** Cumb
41 L4 **Dalton** D & G
38 F6 **Dalton-in-Furness** Cumb
54 A5 **Dalwhinnie** Highld
8 B4 **Damerham** Hants
16 F6 **Danbury** Essex
38 C2 **Darlington** Darltn
43 J5 **Darras Hall** Nthumb
34 B5 **Darrington** Wakefd
10 D2 **Dartford** Kent
6 B5 **Dartington** Devon
6 C6 **Dartmouth** Devon
45 J4 **Darvel** E Ayrs
32 F5 **Darwen** Bl w D
15 G6 **Datchet** W & M
59 H5 **Dava** Highld
28 D3 **Davenham** Ches W
23 G4 **Daventry** Nhants
58 F5 **Daviot** Highld
6 C4 **Dawlish** Devon
11 L3 **Deal** Kent
41 L7 **Dearham** Cumb
17 J2 **Debenham** Suffk
22 F6 **Deddington** Oxon
17 H4 **Dedham** Essex
31 H8 **Deeping St James** Lincs
31 H7 **Deeping St Nicholas** Lincs
27 G2 **Deganwy** Conwy
3 G3 **Delabole** Cnwll
27 J3 **Denbigh** Denbgs
33 L6 **Denby Dale** Kirk
15 G5 **Denham** Bucks
46 F7 **Denholm** Border
17 K1 **Dennington** Suffk
50 D8 **Denny** Falk
11 K4 **Densole** Kent
15 K4 **Dent** Cumb
33 H7 **Denton** Tamesd
29 K6 **Derby** C Derb
36 b4 **Derbyhaven** IoM
25 G4 **Dereham** Norfk
24 E3 **Dersingham** Norfk
46 A2 **Dervaig** Ag & B
23 H3 **Desborough** Nhants
22 F1 **Desford** Leics
20 B3 **Devil's Bridge** Cerdgn
13 K5 **Devizes** Wilts
33 L5 **Dewsbury** Kirk
14 L8 **Dial Post** W Susx
14 C5 **Didcot** Oxon
13 J3 **Didmarton** Gloucs
31 G4 **Digby** Lincs
20 L7 **Dilwyn** Herefs
27 G7 **Dinas-Mawddwy** Gwynd
58 E4 **Dingwall** Highld
36 D6 **Dinnington** Rothm
44 C4 **Dippen** Ag & B
17 L2 **Diseworth** Leics
38 D6 **Dishforth** N York
29 G2 **Disley** Ches E
25 H7 **Diss** Norfk
10 B6 **Ditchling** E Susx
6 C6 **Dittisham** Devon
21 K2 **Ditton Priors** Shrops
3 H4 **Dobwalls** Cnwll
24 E3 **Docking** Norfk
24 B6 **Doddington** Cambs
11 G3 **Doddington** Kent
10 B2 **Doddington** Nthumb
33 L6 **Dodworth** Barns
26 F7 **Dolgellau** Gwynd

50 E6 **Dollar** Clacks
46 B5 **Dolphinton** S Lans
4 E6 **Dolton** Devon
26 F5 **Dolwyddelan** Conwy
34 C6 **Doncaster** Donc
31 H6 **Donington** Lincs
7 K3 **Dorchester** Dorset
14 D4 **Dorchester** Oxon
22 D1 **Dordon** Warwks
58 E5 **Dores** Highld
9 L2 **Dorking** Surrey
57 H6 **Dornie** Highld
59 G1 **Dornoch** Highld
21 J1 **Dorrington** Shrops
21 G6 **Dorstone** Herefs
36 c3 **Douglas** IoM
45 L5 **Douglas** S Lans
65 b3 **Dounby** Ork
50 C6 **Doune** Stirlg
3 L4 **Dousland** Devon
11 L4 **Dover** Kent
29 H6 **Doveridge** Derbys
50 E3 **Dowally** P & K
3 J5 **Downderry** Cnwll
24 D5 **Downham Market** Norfk
8 C4 **Downton** Wilts
22 A5 **Drakes Broughton** Worcs
12 F6 **Draycott** Somset
25 J4 **Drayton** Norfk
14 C4 **Drayton** Oxon
39 J7 **Driffield** E R Yk
52 C5 **Drimnin** Highld
22 A4 **Droitwich** Worcs
29 K3 **Dronfield** Derbys
8 F4 **Droxford** Hants
63 G4 **Drumbeg** Highld
40 C7 **Drummore** D & G
58 D6 **Drumnadrochit** Highld
50 A7 **Drymen** Stirlg
56 D6 **Drynoch** Highld
23 K1 **Duddington** Nhants
22 A2 **Dudley** Dudley
29 K5 **Duffield** Derbys
59 K3 **Duffus** Moray
59 H6 **Dulnain Bridge** Highld
4 L4 **Dulverton** Somset
49 M5 **Dumbarton** W Duns
41 K4 **Dumfries** D & G
42 D7 **Dunbar** E Loth
65 H5 **Dunbeath** Highld
50 D6 **Dunblane** Stirlg
22 F3 **Dunchurch** Warwks
51 J4 **Dundee** C Dund
45 G4 **Dundonald** S Ayrs
57 K1 **Dundonnell** Highld
41 M6 **Dundrennan** D & G
46 B2 **Dunfermline** Fife
50 F3 **Dunkeld** P & K
45 H3 **Dunlop** E Ayrs
65 H2 **Dunnet** Highld
50 F5 **Dunning** P & K
49 K5 **Dunoon** Ag & B
40 C6 **Dunragit** D & G
47 H4 **Duns** Border
41 J4 **Dunscore** D & G
9 K3 **Dunsfold** Surrey
6 B3 **Dunsford** Devon
32 F7 **Dunsop Bridge** Lancs
15 G2 **Dunstable** C Beds
5 J3 **Dunster** Somset
7 K2 **Duntish** Dorset
44 F4 **Dunure** S Ayrs
19 J6 **Dunvant** Swans
56 B3 **Dunvegan** Highld
25 L8 **Dunwich** Suffk
43 K7 **Durham** Dur
63 J2 **Durness** Highld
53 G5 **Duror** Highld
8 C2 **Durrington** Wilts
55 L5 **Durris** Abers
13 H2 **Dursley** Gloucs
16 D3 **Duxford** Cambs
55 M3 **Dyce** C Aber
26 E7 **Dyffryn Ardudwy** Gwynd
11 J5 **Dymchurch** Kent
21 K7 **Dymock** Gloucs

E

42 A4 **Eaglesfield** D & G
45 J3 **Eaglesham** E Rens
15 J5 **Ealing** Gt Lon
33 H3 **Earby** Lancs

21 G5 **Eardisley** Herefs
24 B7 **Earith** Cambs
14 E6 **Earley** Wokham
23 J4 **Earls Barton** Nhants
17 G4 **Earls Colne** Essex
46 F6 **Earlston** Border
25 K6 **Earsham** Norfk
48 F2 **Easdale** Ag & B
9 J4 **Easebourne** W Susx
43 L7 **Easington** Dur
35 K5 **Easington** E R Yk
38 E6 **Easingwold** N York
39 J5 **East Ayton** N York
31 H2 **East Barkwith** Lincs
17 J4 **East Bergholt** Suffk
10 E7 **Eastbourne** E Susx
7 H1 **East Chinnock** Somset
11 H2 **Eastchurch** Kent
8 E6 **East Cowes** IoW
10 D8 **East Dean** E Susx
9 J4 **East Dean** W Susx
30 C7 **East Goscote** Leics
10 C4 **East Grinstead** W Susx
25 G6 **East Harling** Norfk
10 D6 **East Hoathly** E Susx
15 H8 **East Horsley** Surrey
14 C5 **East Ilsley** W Berk
43 J3 **East Kilbride** S Lans
13 J7 **East Knoyle** Wilts
9 H5 **East Lavant** W Susx
8 E4 **Eastleigh** Hants
46 F3 **East Linton** E Loth
7 L4 **East Lulworth** Dorset
17 K2 **Easton** Suffk
6 B7 **East Prawle** Devon
9 K5 **East Preston** W Susx
42 A5 **Eastriggs** D & G
24 D5 **East Rudham** Norfk
11 L3 **Eastry** Kent
46 E3 **East Saltoun** E Loth
30 D5 **East Stoke** Notts
9 H6 **East Wittering** W Susx
38 B5 **East Witton** N York
29 L5 **Eastwood** Notts
23 L4 **Eaton Socon** Cambs
12 C1 **Ebbw Vale** Blae G
43 H6 **Ebchester** Dur
41 M4 **Ecclefechan** D & G
47 H5 **Eccles** Border
28 F6 **Eccleshall** Staffs
55 K4 **Echt** Abers
29 J4 **Eckington** Derbys
22 A6 **Eckington** Worcs
58 F2 **Edderton** Highld
46 C5 **Eddleston** Border
10 C4 **Edenbridge** Kent
56 D4 **Edinbane** Highld
12 E3 **Edinburgh** C Edin
31 H3 **Edlington** Lincs
43 H6 **Edmundbyers** Dur
47 G6 **Ednam** Border
30 C3 **Edwinstowe** Notts
55 J7 **Edzell** Angus
15 H7 **Effingham** Surrey
4 F6 **Eggesford** Devon
37 M2 **Eggleston** Dur
15 G6 **Egham** Surrey
47 K7 **Eglingham** Nthumb
18 E3 **Eglwyswrw** Pembks
36 D3 **Egremont** Cumb
39 H3 **Egton Bridge** N York
20 D4 **Elan Village** Powys
59 K3 **Elgin** Moray
56 E7 **Elgol** Highld
11 J4 **Elham** Kent
51 K6 **Elie** Fife
30 D3 **Elkesley** Notts
33 K1 **Elkstone** Gloucs
33 K5 **Elland** Calder
28 B6 **Ellesmere** Shrops
28 B3 **Ellesmere Port** Ches W
25 K6 **Ellingham** Norfk
61 G6 **Ellon** Abers
34 F4 **Elloughton** E R Yk
17 H5 **Elmstead Market** Essex
43 G3 **Elsdon** Nthumb
46 B5 **Elsrickle** S Lans
9 J2 **Elstead** Surrey
15 J4 **Elstree** Herts
37 G3 **Elterwater** Cumb
16 B2 **Eltisley** Cambs
23 L2 **Elton** Cambs
24 F7 **Elveden** Suffk
14 E7 **Elvetham Heath** Hants
34 D3 **Elvington** C York
5 J4 **Elworthy** Somset
24 C7 **Ely** Cambs

47 M7 **Embleton** Nthumb
64 E8 **Embo** Highld
30 E4 **Empingham** Rutlnd
9 H5 **Emsworth** Hants
22 E4 **Enderby** Leics
15 K4 **Enfield** Gt Lon
36 D2 **Ennerdale Bridge** Cumb
14 B2 **Enstone** Oxon
16 C6 **Epping** Essex
15 J7 **Epsom** Surrey
34 E6 **Epworth** N Linc
58 E6 **Errogie** Highld
51 H4 **Errol** P & K
20 E6 **Erwood** Powys
15 H7 **Esher** Surrey
36 E4 **Eskdale Green** Cumb
42 A3 **Eskdalemuir** D & G
31 G8 **Essendine** Rutlnd
15 J3 **Essendon** Herts
38 E2 **Eston** R & Cl
47 J6 **Etal** Nthumb
10 F5 **Etchingham** E Susx
15 G6 **Eton** W & M
22 D5 **Ettington** Warwks
46 D7 **Ettrick** Border
46 E7 **Ettrickbridge** Border
58 E3 **Evanton** Highld
13 G7 **Evercreech** Somset
14 E7 **Eversley** Hants
22 B6 **Evesham** Worcs
13 K2 **Ewen** Gloucs
9 K2 **Ewhurst** Surrey
21 H7 **Ewyas Harold** Herefs
5 H5 **Exbridge** Somset
6 C3 **Exeter** Devon
5 H4 **Exford** Somset
6 C3 **Exminster** Devon
6 D4 **Exmouth** Devon
23 M1 **Eye** C Pete
25 H7 **Eye** Suffk
47 J4 **Eyemouth** Border
10 D2 **Eynsford** Kent
14 B3 **Eynsham** Oxon

9 L5 **Findon** W Susx
23 J3 **Finedon** Nhants
17 H1 **Finningham** Suffk
34 D6 **Finningley** Donc
65 b4 **Finstown** Ork
50 B7 **Firle** Stirlg
48 C2 **Fionnphort** Ag & B
10 D7 **Firle** E Susx
8 F6 **Fishbourne** IoW
18 C3 **Fishguard** Pembks
9 K4 **Fittleworth** W Susx
5 K4 **Fitzhead** Somset
7 c2 **Five Oaks** Jersey
61 c6 **Fladdabister** Shet
39 L6 **Flamborough** E R Yk
15 H3 **Flamstead** Herts
14 F7 **Fleet** Hants
32 C3 **Fleetwood** Lancs
41 K7 **Flimby** Cumb
27 K3 **Flint** Flints
23 K6 **Flitwick** C Beds
39 K5 **Flixton** N York
23 G4 **Flore** Nhants
59 L4 **Fochabers** Moray
11 K5 **Folkestone** Kent
31 G6 **Folkingham** Lincs
7 L1 **Fontmell Magna** Dorset
9 J5 **Fontwell** W Susx
47 J6 **Ford** Nthumb
10 D4 **Fordcombe** Kent
8 C4 **Fordingbridge** Hants
55 K6 **Fordoun** Abers
11 J3 **Fordwich** Kent
6 a2 **Forest** Guern
10 C5 **Forest Row** E Susx
51 J2 **Forfar** Angus
32 C6 **Formby** Sefton
59 J4 **Forres** Moray
58 C7 **Fort Augustus** Highld
50 F5 **Forteviot** P & K
45 M3 **Forth** S Lans
50 C3 **Fortingall** P & K
32 E2 **Forton** Lancs
58 F4 **Fortrose** Highld
7 J4 **Fortuneswell** Dorset
53 H4 **Fort William** Highld
30 E5 **Foston** Lincs
27 L7 **Four Crosses** Powys
9 G5 **Four Marks** Hants
3 G5 **Fowey** Cnwll
21 J6 **Fownhope** Herefs
36 b3 **Foxdale** IoM
58 D7 **Foyers** Highld
17 K2 **Framlingham** Suffk
7 J3 **Frampton** Dorset
10 E5 **Frant** E Susx
61 G3 **Fraserburgh** Abers
24 D8 **Freckenham** Suffk
32 D4 **Freckleton** Lancs
9 H2 **Frensham** Surrey
8 F6 **Freshwater** IoW
25 J7 **Fressingfield** Suffk
65 J2 **Freswick** Highld
39 H7 **Fridaythorpe** E R Yk
14 B4 **Frilford** Oxon
17 K5 **Frinton-on-Sea** Essex
51 K2 **Friockheim** Angus
25 L5 **Fritton** Norfk
36 D2 **Frizington** Cumb
13 H2 **Frocester** Gloucs
28 C3 **Frodsham** Ches W
13 H6 **Frome** Somset
14 A6 **Froxfield** Wilts
9 H5 **Funtington** W Susx
49 J4 **Furnace** Ag & B
29 G2 **Furness Vale** Derbys
16 D2 **Fyfield** Essex
14 B4 **Fyfield** Oxon
60 E5 **Fyvie** Abers

33 H2 **Gargrave** N York
40 F6 **Garlieston** D & G
55 L4 **Garlogie** Abers
42 E7 **Garrigill** Cumb
32 E3 **Garstang** Lancs
20 D5 **Garth** Powys
46 F3 **Garvald** E Loth
58 C3 **Garve** Highld
41 G6 **Gatehouse of Fleet** D & G
43 K5 **Gateshead** Gatesd
22 E5 **Gaydon** Warwks
24 E4 **Gayton** Norfk
31 K6 **Gedney Drove End** Lincs
31 J8 **Gedney Hill** Lincs
4 D4 **Georgeham** Devon
15 G5 **Gerrards Cross** Bucks
46 F3 **Gifford** E Loth
37 L6 **Giggleswick** N York
13 H8 **Gillingham** Dorset
10 F2 **Gillingham** Medway
25 L6 **Gillingham** Norfk
38 B3 **Gilling West** N York
65 J1 **Gills** Highld
50 E4 **Gilmerton** P & K
42 E5 **Gilsland** Nthumb
21 G8 **Gilwern** Mons
16 C2 **Girton** Cambs
40 C3 **Girvan** S Ayrs
33 G2 **Gisburn** Lancs
51 J3 **Glamis** Angus
47 K7 **Glanton** Nthumb
30 B3 **Glapwell** Derbys
20 F6 **Glasbury** Powys
45 J2 **Glasgow** C Glas
23 J1 **Glaston** Rutlnd
12 F7 **Glastonbury** Somset
17 G3 **Glemsford** Suffk
44 A4 **Glenbarr** Ag & B
52 D5 **Glenborrodale** Highld
41 K5 **Glencaple** D & G
53 H5 **Glencoe** Highld
49 H5 **Glendaruel** Ag & B
50 E6 **Glendevon** P & K
50 E5 **Gleneagles** P & K
57 H7 **Glenelg** Highld
51 G5 **Glenfarg** P & K
52 F3 **Glenfinnan** Highld
55 H3 **Glenkindie** Abers
59 K6 **Glenlivet** Moray
40 C6 **Glenluce** D & G
36 b3 **Glen Maye** IoM
37 G2 **Glenridding** Cumb
51 H6 **Glenrothes** Fife
35 G7 **Glentham** Lincs
33 J7 **Glossop** Derbys
21 M7 **Gloucester** Gloucs
27 K6 **Glyn Ceiriog** Wrexhm
19 L6 **Glyncorrwg** Neath
10 C7 **Glynde** E Susx
19 L5 **Glynneath** Neath
20 C8 **Glyntawe** Powys
28 F7 **Gnosall** Staffs
39 H3 **Goathland** N York
12 D7 **Goathurst** Somset
27 L6 **Gobowen** Shrops
9 J2 **Godalming** Surrey
23 M4 **Godmanchester** Cambs
8 F7 **Godshill** IoW
10 C3 **Godstone** Surrey
20 B3 **Goginan** Cerdgn
32 F6 **Golborne** Wigan
17 G6 **Goldhanger** Essex
64 E7 **Golspie** Highld
9 K2 **Gomshall** Surrey
34 E4 **Goole** E R Yk
28 E3 **Goostrey** Ches E
47 G5 **Gordon** Border
46 D4 **Gorebridge** Mdloth
7 c1 **Gorey** Jersey
14 D5 **Goring** Oxon
2 F6 **Gorran Haven** Cnwll
19 J6 **Gorseinon** Swans
31 H6 **Gosberton** Lincs
36 D3 **Gosforth** Cumb
43 J5 **Gosforth** N u Ty
8 F5 **Gosport** Hants
10 F4 **Goudhurst** Kent
49 K5 **Gourock** Inver
19 J6 **Gowerton** Swans
35 H5 **Goxhill** N Linc
11 G2 **Grain** Medway
35 K6 **Grainthorpe** Lincs
2 F6 **Grampound** Cnwll
62 d9 **Gramsdal** W Isls
62 d9 **Gramsdale** W Isls
6 a1 **Grandes Rocques** Guern

36 F2 **Grange** Cumb
50 E8 **Grangemouth** Falk
37 G5 **Grange-over-Sands** Cumb
30 F6 **Grantham** Lincs
59 J6 **Grantown-on-Spey** Highld
47 H4 **Grantshouse** Border
37 G3 **Grasmere** Cumb
38 A6 **Grassington** N York
16 B4 **Graveley** Herts
10 E2 **Gravesend** Kent
10 E1 **Grays** Thurr
38 F3 **Great Ayton** N York
13 H3 **Great Badminton** S Glos
16 E4 **Great Bardfield** Essex
23 L5 **Great Barford** Bed
24 E3 **Great Bircham** Norfk
17 J3 **Great Blakenham** Suffk
30 F8 **Great Casterton** Rutlnd
16 D3 **Great Chesterford** Essex
30 D7 **Great Dalby** Leics
16 E5 **Great Dunmow** Essex
8 B3 **Great Durnford** Wilts
23 L3 **Great Gidding** Cambs
16 B2 **Great Gransden** Cambs
9 H3 **Greatham** Hants
33 G4 **Great Harwood** Lancs
29 G7 **Great Haywood** Staffs
25 G6 **Great Hockham** Norfk
14 F3 **Great Kimble** Bucks
36 F3 **Great Langdale** Cumb
21 L5 **Great Malvern** Worcs
24 E4 **Great Massingham** Norfk
14 F4 **Great Missenden** Bucks
30 F6 **Great Ponton** Lincs
16 E4 **Great Sampford** Essex
28 B3 **Great Saughall** Ches W
14 B6 **Great Shefford** W Berk
16 C3 **Great Shelford** Cambs
38 D3 **Great Smeaton** N York
22 E7 **Great Tew** Oxon
4 E5 **Great Torrington** Devon
17 G8 **Great Wakering** Essex
16 E6 **Great Waltham** Essex
21 L4 **Great Witley** Worcs
25 L5 **Great Yarmouth** Norfk
16 F4 **Great Yeldham** Essex
27 K3 **Greenfield** Flints
38 E7 **Green Hammerton** N York
42 E5 **Greenhead** Nthumb
38 B6 **Greenhow Hill** N York
47 G5 **Greenlaw** Border
50 D6 **Greenloaning** P & K
49 L5 **Greenock** Inver
36 F5 **Greenodd** Cumb
30 F7 **Greetham** Rutlnd
27 L4 **Gresford** Wrexhm
38 B3 **Greta Bridge** Dur
42 B5 **Gretna** D & G
42 B5 **Gretna Green** D & G
42 C8 **Greystoke** Cumb
35 J5 **Grimsby** NE Lin
31 G7 **Grimsthorpe** Lincs
29 J3 **Grindleford** Derbys
34 E7 **Gringley on the Hill** Notts
30 B8 **Groby** Leics
21 H7 **Grosmont** Mons
7 c2 **Grouville** Jersey
14 B5 **Grove** Oxon
51 J5 **Guardbridge** Fife
11 G6 **Guestling Green** E Susx
9 K2 **Guildford** Surrey
38 F2 **Guisborough** R & Cl
33 K3 **Guiseley** Leeds
25 G4 **Guist** Norfk
46 E2 **Gullane** E Loth
34 E5 **Gunness** N Linc
3 K4 **Gunnislake** Cnwll
30 D5 **Gunthorpe** Notts
8 E6 **Gurnard** IoW
8 A5 **Gussage All Saints** Dorset
61 d2 **Gutcher** Shet
24 B5 **Guyhirn** Cambs
2 D7 **Gweek** Cnwll
27 K4 **Gwernymynydd** Flints

2 C6 **Gwithian** Cnwll
27 J5 **Gwyddelwern** Denbgs

H

65 b3 **Hackland** Ork
39 J4 **Hackness** N York
15 K5 **Hackney** Gt Lon
14 E3 **Haddenham** Bucks
24 C7 **Haddenham** Cambs
46 F3 **Haddington** E Loth
25 L6 **Haddiscoe** Norfk
17 H3 **Hadleigh** Suffk
10 E4 **Hadlow** Kent
31 J3 **Hagworthingham** Lincs
10 E7 **Hailsham** E Susx
5 J6 **Halberton** Devon
25 K6 **Hales** Norfk
22 A3 **Halesowen** Dudley
25 K7 **Halesworth** Suffk
33 K4 **Halifax** Calder
65 G2 **Halkirk** Highld
16 F4 **Halstead** Essex
10 D3 **Halstead** Kent
42 E5 **Haltwhistle** Nthumb
6 B6 **Halwell** Devon
4 D7 **Halwill Junction** Devon
9 G4 **Hambledon** Hants
8 E5 **Hamble-le-Rice** Hants
32 D3 **Hambleton** Lancs
45 K3 **Hamilton** S Lans
15 J6 **Hammersmith** Gt Lon
14 C6 **Hampstead Norreys** W Berk
38 C7 **Hampsthwaite** N York
14 B7 **Hamstead Marshall** W Berk
11 H5 **Hamstreet** Kent
10 B5 **Handcross** W Susx
28 C4 **Handley** Ches W
28 F5 **Hanley** C Stke
25 K3 **Happisburgh** Norfk
6 B6 **Harbertonford** Devon
13 H1 **Hardwicke** Gloucs
16 C4 **Hare Street** Herts
33 L3 **Harewood** Leeds
21 J7 **Harewood End** Herefs
26 E6 **Harlech** Gwynd
25 J7 **Harleston** Norfk
56 C5 **Harlosh** Highld
16 C6 **Harlow** Essex
2 E4 **Harlyn** Cnwll
61 d1 **Haroldswick** Shet
15 H3 **Harpenden** Herts
33 L2 **Harrogate** N York
23 K5 **Harrold** Bed
15 H5 **Harrow** Gt Lon
16 C3 **Harston** Cambs
43 H3 **Hartburn** Nthumb
17 G3 **Hartest** Suffk
10 D5 **Hartfield** E Susx
29 H4 **Hartington** Derbys
4 C5 **Hartland** Devon
43 M8 **Hartlepool** Hartpl
14 E7 **Hartley Wintney** Hants
21 L7 **Hartpury** Gloucs
22 B5 **Harvington** Worcs
17 K4 **Harwich** Essex
22 D4 **Haseley** Warwks
9 J3 **Haslemere** Surrey
10 F7 **Hastings** E Susx
12 D8 **Hatch Beauchamp** Somset
34 D5 **Hatfield** Donc
15 J3 **Hatfield** Herts
16 D5 **Hatfield Broad Oak** Essex
16 D5 **Hatfield Heath** Essex
16 F6 **Hatfield Peverel** Essex
4 E6 **Hatherleigh** Devon
30 B7 **Hathern** Leics
29 J2 **Hathersage** Derbys
61 H5 **Hatton** Abers
9 G5 **Havant** Hants
8 F6 **Havenstreet** IoW
18 C5 **Haverfordwest** Pembks
16 E3 **Haverhill** Suffk
27 L3 **Hawarden** Flints
37 L4 **Hawes** N York
46 F7 **Hawick** Border
16 F3 **Hawkedon** Suffk
10 F5 **Hawkhurst** Kent
11 K4 **Hawkinge** Kent

37 G4 **Hawkshead** Cumb
38 E4 **Hawnby** N York
33 J3 **Haworth** C Brad
38 F7 **Haxby** C York
34 E6 **Haxey** N Linc
42 F5 **Haydon Bridge** Nthumb
2 C6 **Hayle** Cnwll
21 G6 **Hay-on-Wye** Powys
10 B6 **Haywards Heath** W Susx
28 F2 **Hazel Grove** Stockp
24 D3 **Heacham** Norfk
11 G4 **Headcorn** Kent
29 L5 **Heanor** Derbys
29 L5 **Heath** Derbys
10 E6 **Heathfield** E Susx
29 G8 **Heath Hayes & Wimblebury** Staffs
31 G5 **Heckington** Lincs
8 E4 **Hedge End** Hants
29 G8 **Hednesford** Staffs
35 H4 **Hedon** E R Yk
49 L5 **Helensburgh** Ag & B
37 L7 **Hellifield** N York
17 K2 **Helmingham** Suffk
65 G6 **Helmsdale** Highld
38 F5 **Helmsley** N York
31 G5 **Helpringham** Lincs
28 C3 **Helsby** Ches W
2 C7 **Helston** Cnwll
15 H3 **Hemel Hempstead** Herts
25 J6 **Hempnall** Norfk
25 L4 **Hemsby** Norfk
34 B5 **Hemsworth** Wakefd
5 K6 **Hemyock** Devon
19 J6 **Hendy** Carmth
9 L4 **Henfield** W Susx
16 D4 **Henham** Essex
22 C4 **Henley-in-Arden** Warwks
14 E5 **Henley-on-Thames** Oxon
27 J3 **Henllan** Denbgs
23 L6 **Henlow** C Beds
25 L7 **Henstead** Suffk
7 K1 **Henstridge** Somset
21 J6 **Hereford** Herefs
14 C6 **Hermitage** W Berk
11 J2 **Herne Bay** Kent
11 K3 **Hersden** Kent
10 E6 **Herstmonceux** E Susx
15 K3 **Hertford** Herts
35 G4 **Hessle** E R Yk
27 L2 **Heswall** Wirral
25 H5 **Hethersett** Norfk
37 H5 **Heversham** Cumb
43 G5 **Hexham** Nthumb
3 M4 **Hexworthy** Devon
3 K6 **Heybrook Bay** Devon
37 G7 **Heysham** Lancs
13 J6 **Heytesbury** Wilts
35 G6 **Hibaldstow** N Linc
10 B6 **Hickstead** W Susx
23 K4 **Higham Ferrers** Nhants
4 E6 **Highampton** Devon
37 J6 **High Bentham** N York
12 D6 **Highbridge** Somset
14 B7 **Highclere** Hants
28 D7 **High Ercall** Wrekin
2 b1 **Higher Town** IoS
11 G5 **High Halden** Kent
42 C7 **High Hesket** Cumb
21 L3 **Highley** Shrops
16 E5 **High Roding** Essex
13 M3 **Highworth** Swindn
14 F4 **High Wycombe** Bucks
10 D4 **Hildenborough** Kent
11 H5 **Hill Brow** Hants
59 G2 **Hill of Fearn** Highld
61 b3 **Hillswick** Shet
13 K4 **Hilmarton** Wilts
22 E2 **Hinckley** Leics
39 G2 **Hinderwell** N York
13 J7 **Hindon** Wilts
25 G5 **Hingham** Norfk
38 B4 **Hipswell** N York
12 A2 **Hirwaun** Rhondd
16 C5 **Histon** Cambs
17 H3 **Hitcham** Suffk
23 M7 **Hitchin** Herts
17 G7 **Hockley** Essex
23 L5 **Hockliffe** C Beds
15 K3 **Hoddesdon** Herts
28 D6 **Hodnet** Shrops
31 L3 **Hogsthorpe** Lincs
31 J7 **Holbeach** Lincs

3 L5 **Holbeton** Devon
17 J4 **Holbrook** Suffk
8 E5 **Holbury** Hants
24 F2 **Holkham** Norfk
11 G3 **Hollingbourne** Kent
9 L2 **Holmbury St Mary** Surrey
28 E3 **Holmes Chapel** Ches E
34 E3 **Holme upon Spalding Moor** E R Yk
33 K6 **Holmfirth** Kirk
36 D4 **Holmrook** Cumb
6 A5 **Holne** Devon
4 C6 **Holsworthy** Devon
25 H3 **Holt** Norfk
13 J5 **Holt** Wilts
28 B4 **Holt** Wrexhm
21 L4 **Holt Heath** Worcs
35 J6 **Holton le Clay** Lincs
47 L5 **Holy Island** Nthumb
45 L2 **Holytown** N Lans
7 J2 **Holywell** Dorset
27 K3 **Holywell** Flints
25 J7 **Homersfield** Suffk
25 H5 **Honingham** Norfk
24 F7 **Honington** Suffk
6 E2 **Honiton** Devon
14 E7 **Hook** Hants
10 F2 **Hoo St Werburgh** Medway
29 J2 **Hope** Derbys
6 A7 **Hope** Devon
27 L4 **Hope** Flints
21 J2 **Hope Bowdler** Shrops
59 K3 **Hopeman** Moray
21 J5 **Hope under Dinmore** Herefs
25 M5 **Hopton on Sea** Norfk
10 D6 **Horam** E Susx
10 B4 **Horley** Surrey
37 J6 **Hornby** Lancs
31 H3 **Horncastle** Lincs
9 G4 **Horndean** Hants
4 D5 **Horns Cross** Devon
35 H3 **Hornsea** E R Yk
3 L4 **Horrabridge** Devon
25 L4 **Horsey** Norfk
9 L3 **Horsham** W Susx
43 H5 **Horsley** Nthumb
8 B5 **Horton** Dorset
6 F1 **Horton** Somset
14 D3 **Horton-cum-Studley** Oxon
37 L6 **Horton in Ribblesdale** N York
32 F5 **Horwich** Bolton
30 C7 **Hoton** Leics
43 K6 **Houghton-le-Spring** Sundld
23 G1 **Houghton on the Hill** Leics
15 H6 **Hounslow** Gt Lon
65 b4 **Houton** Ork
10 B7 **Hove** Br & H
38 F5 **Hovingham** N York
34 E4 **Howden** E R Yk
25 J7 **Hoxne** Suffk
32 B7 **Hoylake** Wirral
34 B6 **Hoyland Nether** Barns
30 B5 **Hucknall** Notts
33 K5 **Huddersfield** Kirk
2 a2 **Hugh Town** IoS
35 J6 **Humberston** NE Lin
46 E4 **Humbie** E Loth
47 G5 **Hume** Border
14 B6 **Hungerford** W Berk
39 K5 **Hunmanby** N York
24 D2 **Hunstanton** Norfk
23 M3 **Huntingdon** Cambs
21 L7 **Huntley** Gloucs
60 C5 **Huntly** Abers
8 E4 **Hursley** Hants
8 E2 **Hurstbourne Priors** Hants
14 B7 **Hurstbourne Tarrant** Hants
10 F5 **Hurst Green** E Susx
32 F3 **Hurst Green** Lancs
10 B6 **Hurstpierpoint** W Susx
38 C3 **Hurworth-on-Tees** Darltn
23 G2 **Husbands Bosworth** Leics
23 K6 **Husborne Crawley** C Beds
31 L3 **Huttoft** Lincs
39 G4 **Hutton-le-Hole** N York
33 H7 **Hyde** Tamesd
48 D3 **Hynish** Ag & B

8 E5 **Hythe** Hants
11 J5 **Hythe** Kent

I

29 K8 **Ibstock** Leics
6 C4 **Ideford** Devon
12 F8 **Ilchester** Somset
4 E3 **Ilfracombe** Devon
29 L5 **Ilkeston** Derbys
33 K3 **Ilkley** C Brad
7 G1 **Ilminster** Somset
35 H5 **Immingham** NE Lin
35 H5 **Immingham Dock** NE Lin
63 H5 **Inchnadamph** Highld
16 E7 **Ingatestone** Essex
30 F2 **Ingham** Lincs
37 K6 **Ingleton** N York
31 L3 **Ingoldmells** Lincs
22 B5 **Inkberrow** Worcs
49 K6 **Innellan** Ag & B
46 D6 **Innerleithen** Border
60 D6 **Insch** Abers
54 C4 **Insh** Highld
4 D4 **Instow** Devon
61 G3 **Inverallochy** Abers
64 C7 **Inveran** Highld
49 J3 **Inveraray** Ag & B
57 H2 **Inverasdale** Highld
55 L6 **Inverbervie** Abers
53 K2 **Invergarry** Highld
58 F3 **Invergordon** Highld
51 H4 **Invergowrie** P & K
57 J6 **Inverinate** Highld
51 L2 **Inverkeilor** Angus
46 B2 **Inverkeithing** Fife
60 D6 **Inverkeithny** Abers
49 K6 **Inverkip** Inver
58 D7 **Invermoriston** Highld
58 F5 **Inverness** Highld
55 L3 **Inverurie** Abers
6 B5 **Ipplepen** Devon
29 G5 **Ipstones** Staffs
17 J3 **Ipswich** Suffk
23 J4 **Irchester** Nhants
42 A7 **Ireby** Cumb
21 K1 **Ironbridge** Wrekin
23 K3 **Irthlingborough** Nhants
45 G4 **Irvine** N Ayrs
40 F7 **Isle of Whithorn** D & G
57 G2 **Isleornsay** Highld
15 K5 **Islington** Gt Lon
8 F3 **Itchen Abbas** Hants
15 G5 **Iver** Bucks
15 G3 **Ivinghoe** Bucks
3 M5 **Ivybridge** Devon
11 G2 **Iwade** Kent
7 L1 **Iwerne Minster** Dorset
25 G8 **Ixworth** Suffk

J

43 K5 **Jarrow** S Tyne
47 G7 **Jedburgh** Border
6 b2 **Jerbourg** Guern
12 F8 **Jevington** E Susx
65 J1 **John o' Groats** Highld
55 L7 **Johnshaven** Abers
18 C5 **Johnston** Pembks
49 M6 **Johnstone** Rens
36 c1 **Jurby** IoM

K

49 H6 **Kames** Ag & B
35 H5 **Keelby** Lincs
30 B6 **Kegworth** Leics
33 J3 **Keighley** C Brad
65 J2 **Keiss** Highld
60 B4 **Keith** Moray
37 L3 **Keld** N York
30 D4 **Kelham** Notts
47 G6 **Kelso** Border
17 G5 **Kelvedon** Essex
13 K2 **Kemble** Gloucs
55 K3 **Kemnay** Abers
23 K5 **Kempston** Bed
37 H4 **Kendal** Cumb
22 D3 **Kenilworth** Warwks
50 D3 **Kenmore** P & K
49 G6 **Kennacraig** Ag & B

6 C3 **Kennford** Devon
25 G7 **Kenninghall** Norfk
53 G5 **Kentallen** Highld
16 F2 **Kentford** Suffk
6 C4 **Kenton** Devon
20 F2 **Kerry** Powys
25 L6 **Kessingland** Suffk
36 F2 **Keswick** Cumb
23 J3 **Kettering** Nhants
37 M6 **Kettlewell** N York
23 K1 **Ketton** Rutlnd
10 B6 **Keymer** W Susx
13 G4 **Keynsham** BaNES
23 K3 **Keyston** Cambs
30 C6 **Keyworth** Notts
23 G2 **Kibworth Harcourt** Leics
21 M3 **Kidderminster** Worcs
14 C3 **Kidlington** Oxon
28 F4 **Kidsgrove** Staffs
19 G5 **Kidwelly** Carmth
42 D3 **Kielder** Nthumb
48 F6 **Kilberry** Ag & B
45 G3 **Kilbirnie** N Ayrs
29 K5 **Kilburn** Derbys
38 E5 **Kilburn** N York
44 E3 **Kilchattan** Ag & B
52 C4 **Kilchoan** Highld
49 J2 **Kilchrenan** Ag & B
49 K5 **Kilcreggan** Ag & B
38 F3 **Kildale** N York
55 H3 **Kildrummy** Abers
33 J3 **Kildwick** N York
49 H5 **Kilfinan** Ag & B
18 E5 **Kilgetty** Pembks
39 K6 **Kilham** E R Yk
44 B5 **Kilkenzie** Ag & B
4 C6 **Kilkhampton** Cnwll
50 B7 **Killearn** Stirlg
54 D7 **Killiecrankie** P & K
50 B4 **Killin** Stirlg
49 L6 **Kilmacolm** Inver
51 J5 **Kilmany** Fife
45 H4 **Kilmarnock** E Ayrs
49 G4 **Kilmartin** Ag & B
45 H4 **Kilmaurs** E Ayrs
49 G3 **Kilmelford** Ag & B
58 D5 **Kilmorack** Highld
49 G2 **Kilninver** Ag & B
50 C8 **Kilsyth** N Lans
5 K3 **Kilve** Somset
45 G4 **Kilwinning** N Ayrs
25 H5 **Kimberley** Norfk
23 L4 **Kimbolton** Cambs
64 E5 **Kinbrace** Highld
50 E7 **Kincardine** Fife
55 J4 **Kincardine O'Neil** Abers
54 C4 **Kincraig** Highld
22 E5 **Kineton** Warwks
51 K5 **Kingsbarns** Fife
6 B7 **Kingsbridge** Devon
22 D2 **Kingsbury** Warwks
14 C7 **Kingsclere** Hants
23 K1 **King's Cliffe** Nhants
11 L4 **Kingsdown** Kent
9 L3 **Kingsfold** W Susx
6 C5 **Kingskerswell** Devon
21 H4 **Kingsland** Herefs
15 H4 **Kings Langley** Herts
29 G5 **Kingsley** Staffs
24 D4 **King's Lynn** Norfk
6 a2 **King's Mills** Guern
11 H4 **Kingsnorth** Kent
8 D3 **King's Somborne** Hants
7 K2 **King's Stag** Dorset
13 H2 **King's Stanley** Gloucs
6 C4 **Kingsteignton** Devon
21 H6 **Kingstone** Herefs
59 L3 **Kingston on Spey** Moray
35 G4 **Kingston upon Hull** C KuH
15 J6 **Kingston upon Thames** Gt Lon
6 C6 **Kingswear** Devon
8 E3 **Kings Worthy** Hants
21 G5 **Kington** Herefs
54 B4 **Kingussie** Highld
63 H3 **Kinlochbervie** Highld
53 G3 **Kinlocheil** Highld
57 J3 **Kinlochewe** Highld
50 C2 **Kinloch Rannoch** P & K
59 J3 **Kinloss** Moray
50 F6 **Kinross** P & K
14 B6 **Kintbury** W Berk

55 L3 **Kintore** Abers
50 C7 **Kippen** Stirlg
39 G5 **Kirby Misperton** N York
22 F1 **Kirby Muxloe** Leics
61 c6 **Kirkabister** Shet
41 K6 **Kirkbean** D & G
42 A6 **Kirkbride** Cumb
33 K5 **Kirkburton** Kirk
32 D6 **Kirkby** Knows
30 B4 **Kirkby in Ashfield** Notts
37 J5 **Kirkby Lonsdale** Cumb
38 C5 **Kirkby Malzeard** N York
39 G5 **Kirkbymoorside** N York
37 K3 **Kirkby Stephen** Cumb
51 H7 **Kirkcaldy** Fife
40 B5 **Kirkcolm** D & G
40 D5 **Kirkcowan** D & G
41 G6 **Kirkcudbright** D & G
32 D4 **Kirkham** Lancs
58 E5 **Kirkhill** Highld
40 E6 **Kirkinner** D & G
45 K1 **Kirkintilloch** E Duns
29 K6 **Kirk Langley** Derbys
36 b2 **Kirk Michael** IoM
50 F2 **Kirkmichael** P & K
45 G6 **Kirkmichael** S Ayrs
47 J6 **Kirknewton** Nthumb
42 D7 **Kirkoswald** Cumb
44 F6 **Kirkoswald** S Ayrs
42 B5 **Kirkpatrick-Fleming** D & G
55 L4 **Kirkton of Skene** Abers
65 c4 **Kirkwall** Ork
43 H4 **Kirkwhelpington** Nthumb
51 J2 **Kirriemuir** Angus
31 J6 **Kirton** Lincs
34 F6 **Kirton in Lindsey** N Linc
23 H4 **Kislingbury** Nhants
38 D7 **Knaresborough** N York
42 E6 **Knarsdale** Nthumb
15 J2 **Knebworth** Herts
21 G3 **Knighton** Powys
21 L5 **Knightwick** Worcs
63 H6 **Knockan** Highld
27 L7 **Knockin** Shrops
34 C4 **Knottingley** Wakefd
14 F5 **Knowl Hill** W & M
28 E3 **Knutsford** Ches E
57 G6 **Kyleakin** Highld
57 G6 **Kyle of Lochalsh** Highld
57 G7 **Kylerhea** Highld

L

35 H6 **Laceby** NE Lin
2 E5 **Ladock** Cnwll
51 H5 **Ladybank** Fife
54 A5 **Laggan** Highld
7 a1 **La Greve de Lecq** Jersey
62 E8 **Laide** Highld
64 C6 **Lairg** Highld
52 E7 **Lakenheath** Suffk
10 E5 **Lamberhurst** Kent
14 B6 **Lambourn** W Berk
3 K3 **Lamerton** Devon
46 A6 **Lamington** S Lans
44 D5 **Lamlash** N Ayrs
19 J2 **Lampeter** Cerdgn
23 H3 **Lamport** Nhants
45 M4 **Lanark** S Lans
37 H6 **Lancaster** Lancs
43 J6 **Lanchester** Dur
9 L5 **Lancing** W Susx
6 b1 **L'Ancresse** Guern
3 J5 **Landrake** Cnwll
30 E8 **Langham** Rutlnd
42 B4 **Langholm** D & G
12 E8 **Langport** Somset
38 A3 **Langthwaite** N York
39 J6 **Langtoft** E R Yk
8 A7 **Langton Matravers** Dorset
42 D7 **Langwathby** Cumb
31 G3 **Langworth** Lincs
3 G4 **Lanivet** Cnwll

5 G6 **Lapford** Devon
51 J6 **Largoward** Fife
44 F2 **Largs** N Ayrs
45 L3 **Larkhall** S Lans
8 B2 **Larkhill** Wilts
39 G4 **Lastingham** N York
17 G7 **Latchingdon** Essex
65 H4 **Latheron** Highld
46 F5 **Lauder** Border
18 F5 **Laugharne** Carmth
3 J3 **Launceston** Cnwll
55 K6 **Laurencekirk** Abers
41 G5 **Laurieston** D & G
17 G3 **Lavenham** Suffk
50 C3 **Lawers** P & K
36 c3 **Laxey** IoM
25 K8 **Laxfield** Suffk
42 D7 **Lazonby** Cumb
30 F5 **Leadenham** Lincs
16 E6 **Leaden Roding** Essex
43 J6 **Leadgate** Dur
45 M6 **Leadhills** S Lans
22 D4 **Leamington Spa** Warwks
15 J7 **Leatherhead** Surrey
13 M2 **Lechlade on Thames** Gloucs
21 L6 **Ledbury** Herefs
4 E3 **Lee** Devon
21 J1 **Leebotwood** Shrops
33 L4 **Leeds** Leeds
29 G4 **Leek** Staffs
38 C4 **Leeming Bar** N York
8 F5 **Lee-on-the-Solent** Hants
31 J2 **Legbourne** Lincs
23 G1 **Leicester** C Leic
10 D4 **Leigh** Kent
32 F6 **Leigh** Wigan
21 L5 **Leigh Sinton** Worcs
23 J7 **Leighton Buzzard** C Beds
21 H3 **Leintwardine** Herefs
17 M2 **Leiston** Suffk
2 C6 **Lelant** Cnwll
40 C3 **Lendalfoot** S Ayrs
11 G3 **Lenham** Kent
50 B8 **Lennoxtown** E Duns
21 J4 **Leominster** Herefs
6 a2 **L'Eree** Guern
61 c6 **Lerwick** Shet
60 D6 **Leslie** Abers
51 H6 **Leslie** Fife
45 L4 **Lesmahagow** S Lans
40 B5 **Leswalt** D & G
7 a1 **L'Etacq** Jersey
16 B4 **Letchworth Garden City** Herts
51 K3 **Letham** Angus
18 C4 **Letterston** Pembks
51 J5 **Leuchars** Fife
35 H3 **Leven** E R Yk
51 J6 **Leven** Fife
37 H5 **Levens** Cumb
62 e7 **Leverburgh** W Isls
10 C7 **Lewes** E Susx
38 B4 **Leyburn** N York
32 E5 **Leyland** Lancs
11 H2 **Leysdown-on-Sea** Kent
59 L3 **Lhanbryde** Moray
46 A5 **Libberton** S Lans
29 H8 **Lichfield** Staffs
16 F2 **Lidgate** Suffk
3 J3 **Lifton** Devon
15 G7 **Lightwater** Surrey
46 F7 **Lilliesleaf** Border
13 H5 **Limpley Stoke** Wilts
30 F3 **Lincoln** Lincs
37 G5 **Lindale** Cumb
10 C4 **Lingfield** Surrey
46 A3 **Linlithgow** W Loth
16 D3 **Linton** Cambs
10 F4 **Linton** Kent
9 H3 **Liphook** Hants
3 H4 **Liskeard** Cnwll
9 H3 **Liss** Hants
31 G2 **Lissington** Lincs
24 F4 **Litcham** Norfk
14 C7 **Litchfield** Hants
16 D3 **Little Abington** Cambs
15 K3 **Little Berkhamsted** Herts
33 H5 **Littleborough** Rochdl
23 J6 **Little Brickhill** M Keyn
30 F7 **Little Bytham** Lincs
17 J5 **Little Clacton** Essex
15 G3 **Little Gaddesden** Herts

9 K5 **Littlehampton** W Susx
24 D6 **Littleport** Cambs
21 H2 **Little Stretton** Shrops
4 E5 **Little Torrington** Devon
25 G3 **Little Walsingham** Norfk
32 C7 **Liverpool** Lpool
46 B3 **Livingston** W Loth
2 D8 **Lizard** Cnwll
26 C5 **Llanaelhaearn** Gwynd
27 K6 **Llanarmon Dyffryn Ceiriog** Wrexhm
19 H4 **Llanarthne** Carmth
26 E6 **Llanbedr** Gwynd
27 K4 **Llanbedr-Dyffryn-Clwyd** Denbgs
26 C6 **Llanbedrog** Gwynd
26 E4 **Llanberis** Gwynd
20 F3 **Llanbister** Powys
20 D1 **Llanbrynmair** Powys
19 H5 **Llanddarog** Carmth
27 H6 **Llandderfel** Gwynd
27 H3 **Llanddulas** Conwy
19 J4 **Llandeilo** Carmth
20 E2 **Llandinam** Powys
18 E4 **Llandissilio** Pembks
19 K3 **Llandovery** Carmth
20 B2 **Llandre** Cerdgn
27 J6 **Llandrillo** Denbgs
20 E4 **Llandrindod Wells** Powys
27 L7 **Llandrinio** Powys
27 G2 **Llandudno** Conwy
26 D4 **Llandwrog** Gwynd
19 J5 **Llandybie** Carmth
19 G3 **Llandysul** Cerdgn
19 H6 **Llanelli** Carmth
26 D2 **Llanerchymedd** IoA
27 J8 **Llanerfyl** Powys
26 C2 **Llanfachraeth** IoA
27 J8 **Llanfair Caereinion** Powys
27 J4 **Llanfair Dyffryn Clwyd** Denbgs
26 F3 **Llanfairfechan** Conwy
26 D3 **Llanfair P G** IoA
27 H3 **Llanfair Talhaiarn** Conwy
21 G3 **Llanfair Waterdine** Shrops
20 A3 **Llanfarian** Cerdgn
27 K7 **Llanfyllin** Powys
27 H8 **Llangadfan** Powys
19 K4 **Llangadog** Carmth
20 D5 **Llangammarch Wells** Powys
27 K7 **Llangedwyn** Powys
26 D3 **Llangefni** IoA
19 L7 **Llangeinor** Brdgnd
19 G3 **Llangeler** Carmth
19 G6 **Llangennith** Swans
27 G3 **Llangernyw** Conwy
26 E2 **Llangoed** IoA
27 K5 **Llangollen** Denbgs
20 F7 **Llangors** Powys
18 F2 **Llangranog** Cerdgn
20 D3 **Llangurig** Powys
20 F7 **Llangynidr** Powys
27 J7 **Llangynog** Powys
20 E7 **Llanhamlach** Powys
19 L7 **Llanharan** Rhondd
20 D2 **Llanidloes** Powys
20 B3 **Llanilar** Cerdgn
26 E3 **Llanllechid** Gwynd
27 H3 **Llannefydd** Conwy
27 J7 **Llanrhaeadr-ym-Mochnant** Powys
19 H6 **Llanrhidian** Swans
20 A4 **Llanrhystud** Cerdgn
26 E4 **Llanrug** Gwynd
27 G4 **Llanrwst** Conwy
27 G3 **Llansanffraid Glan Conwy** Conwy
27 H3 **Llansannan** Conwy
19 H1 **Llansantffraid** Cerdgn
27 K7 **Llansantffraid-ym-Mechain** Powys
19 J3 **Llansawel** Carmth
19 L5 **Llansteffan** Carmth
21 G7 **Llanthony** Mons
12 B3 **Llantrisant** Rhondd
5 J1 **Llantwit Major** V Glam
27 G6 **Llanuwchllyn** Gwynd
21 H8 **Llanwenarth** Mons
21 G7 **Llanvihangel Crucorney** Mons
27 J7 **Llanwddyn** Powys
26 D4 **Llanwnda** Gwynd

19 K3 **Llanwrda** Carmth
20 D5 **Llanwrtyd Wells** Powys
19 H2 **Llanybydder** Carmth
27 L7 **Llanymynech** Powys
26 D6 **Llanystumdwy** Gwynd
27 L4 **Llay** Wrexhm
18 F3 **Llechryd** Cerdgn
26 E8 **Llwyngwril** Gwynd
27 K6 **Llwynmawr** Wrexhm
27 L7 **Llynclys** Shrops
20 F6 **Llyswen** Powys
52 E3 **Lochailort** Highld
52 D6 **Lochaline** Highld
41 K4 **Locharbriggs** D & G
53 H7 **Lochawe** Ag & B
62 c12 **Loch Baghasdail** W Isls
62 c12 **Lochboisdale** W Isls
52 D7 **Lochbuie** Ag & B
57 H5 **Lochcarron** Highld
52 E7 **Lochdonhead** Ag & B
50 B4 **Lochearnhead** Stirlg
49 H4 **Lochgair** Ag & B
49 G4 **Lochgilphead** Ag & B
49 K3 **Lochgoilhead** Ag & B
63 G5 **Lochinver** Highld
41 L4 **Lochmaben** D & G
62 d8 **Lochmaddy** W Isls
62 d8 **Loch nam Madadh** W Isls
44 D3 **Lochranza** N Ayrs
45 G2 **Lochwinnoch** Rens
41 L4 **Lockerbie** D & G
39 H4 **Lockton** N York
25 K6 **Loddon** Norfk
38 B6 **Lofthouse** N York
39 G2 **Loftus** R & Cl
15 J5 **London** Gt Lon
15 J4 **London Colney** Herts
12 F4 **Long Ashton** N Som
30 E5 **Long Bennington** Lincs
23 G4 **Long Buckby** Nhants
7 J1 **Longburton** Dorset
22 D6 **Long Compton** Warwks
14 E3 **Long Crendon** Bucks
30 B6 **Long Eaton** Derbys
21 M7 **Longford** Gloucs
47 G4 **Longformacus** Border
43 J2 **Longframlington** Nthumb
8 B6 **Longham** Dorset
43 J3 **Longhorsley** Nthumb
47 M7 **Longhoughton** Nthumb
22 E4 **Long Itchington** Warwks
22 F3 **Long Lawford** Warwks
34 C2 **Long Marston** N York
17 G3 **Long Melford** Suffk
46 E3 **Longniddry** E Loth
21 J1 **Longnor** Shrops
29 H4 **Longnor** Staffs
37 L7 **Long Preston** N York
32 F3 **Longridge** Lancs
45 M2 **Longridge** W Loth
61 G5 **Longside** Abers
25 J6 **Long Stratton** Norfk
31 K7 **Long Sutton** Lincs
12 F8 **Long Sutton** Somset
32 D4 **Longton** Lancs
42 B5 **Longtown** Cumb
21 J2 **Longville in the Dale** Shrops
3 H5 **Looe** Cnwll
59 K3 **Lossiemouth** Moray
3 G5 **Lostwithiel** Cnwll
30 B7 **Loughborough** Leics
31 J2 **Louth** Lincs
30 D5 **Lowdham** Notts
57 H4 **Lower Diabaig** Highld
10 D6 **Lower Dicker** E Susx
28 E3 **Lower Peover** Ches E
22 C7 **Lower Swell** Gloucs
25 M6 **Lowestoft** Suffk
36 E2 **Loweswater** Cumb
23 K3 **Lowick** Nhants
47 K5 **Lowick** Nthumb
37 M4 **Low Row** N York
23 H2 **Lubenham** Leics
35 J7 **Ludborough** Lincs
8 D2 **Ludgershall** Wilts
25 K4 **Ludham** Norfk
21 J3 **Ludlow** Shrops
45 H3 **Lugton** E Ayrs
21 J6 **Lugwardine** Herefs
55 J4 **Lumphanan** Abers
55 H3 **Lumsden** Abers
51 L2 **Lunan** Angus

37 H5 **Lupton** Cumb
49 L4 **Luss** Ag & B
56 C4 **Lusta** Highld
15 H2 **Luton** Luton
22 F2 **Lutterworth** Leics
65 H4 **Lybster** Highld
21 H2 **Lydbury North** Shrops
11 H6 **Lydd** Kent
3 L3 **Lydford** Devon
12 F7 **Lydford on Fosse** Somset
21 G2 **Lydham** Shrops
13 G2 **Lydney** Gloucs
7 G3 **Lyme Regis** Dorset
11 K6 **Lyminge** Kent
8 D6 **Lymington** Hants
28 E2 **Lymm** Warrtn
11 J5 **Lympne** Kent
8 D5 **Lyndhurst** Hants
13 K4 **Lyneham** Wilts
65 b5 **Lyness** Ork
12 E7 **Lyng** Somset
5 G3 **Lynmouth** Devon
4 F3 **Lynton** Devon
21 G5 **Lyonshall** Herefs
32 C4 **Lytham St Anne's** Lancs
39 H3 **Lythe** N York

M

31 K2 **Mablethorpe** Lincs
28 F3 **Macclesfield** Ches E
60 E3 **Macduff** Abers
44 A5 **Machrihanish** Ag & B
20 C1 **Machynlleth** Powys
46 E3 **Macmerry** E Loth
26 F5 **Maentwrog** Gwynd
12 B2 **Maerdy** Rhondd
19 L7 **Maesteg** Brdgnd
32 B6 **Maghull** Sefton
13 H7 **Maiden Bradley** Wilts
6 C5 **Maidencombe** Torbay
14 F5 **Maidenhead** W & M
7 J3 **Maiden Newton** Dorset
10 F3 **Maidstone** Kent
41 K6 **Mainsriddle** D & G
6 A7 **Malborough** Devon
17 G6 **Maldon** Essex
37 L6 **Malham** N York
52 D2 **Mallaig** Highld
27 G8 **Mallwyd** Gwynd
13 J3 **Malmesbury** Wilts
28 C5 **Malpas** Ches W
34 C7 **Maltby** Rothm
39 G6 **Malton** N York
21 L6 **Malvern Wells** Worcs
2 D7 **Manaccan** Cnwll
33 G6 **Manchester** Manch
24 C6 **Manea** Cambs
17 J4 **Manningtree** Essex
18 D6 **Manorbier** Pembks
30 B4 **Mansfield** Notts
2 E5 **Marazanvose** Cnwll
2 B7 **Marazion** Cnwll
24 B6 **March** Cambs
28 B5 **Marchwiel** Wrexhm
10 F4 **Marden** Kent
31 J4 **Mareham le Fen** Lincs
16 E6 **Margaretting** Essex
11 L2 **Margate** Kent
12 E6 **Mark** Somset
10 E5 **Mark Cross** E Susx
22 E1 **Market Bosworth** Leics
31 G8 **Market Deeping** Lincs
28 D6 **Market Drayton** Shrops
23 H2 **Market Harborough** Leics
13 K6 **Market Lavington** Wilts
35 H7 **Market Rasen** Lincs
30 C3 **Market Warsop** Notts
34 F3 **Market Weighton** E R Yk
30 B8 **Markfield** Leics
30 D3 **Markham Moor** Notts
13 G5 **Marksbury** BaNES
17 G5 **Marks Tey** Essex
13 M4 **Marlborough** Wilts
18 B5 **Marloes** Pembks
14 F5 **Marlow** Bucks
7 K1 **Marnhull** Dorset
13 H4 **Marshfield** S Glos
14 D2 **Marsh Gibbon** Bucks

38 F2 **Marske-by-the-Sea** R & Cl
31 G4 **Martin** Lincs
7 J3 **Martinstown** Dorset
17 K3 **Martlesham Heath** Suffk
7 H1 **Martock** Somset
22 E4 **Marton** Warwks
55 K7 **Marykirk** Abers
41 K7 **Maryport** Cumb
3 L3 **Mary Tavy** Devon
55 J5 **Marywell** Abers
38 C5 **Masham** N York
10 E4 **Matfield** Kent
29 K4 **Matlock** Derbys
14 E7 **Mattingley** Hants
45 H5 **Mauchline** E Ayrs
60 F4 **Maud** Abers
36 d2 **Maughold** IoM
23 K6 **Maulden** C Beds
2 E4 **Mawgan Porth** Cnwll
2 D7 **Mawnan Smith** Cnwll
45 G6 **Maybole** S Ayrs
10 E5 **Mayfield** E Susx
29 H5 **Mayfield** Staffs
12 F6 **Meare** Somset
29 K8 **Measham** Leics
9 G3 **Medstead** Hants
4 E6 **Meeth** Devon
27 K8 **Meifod** Powys
51 H3 **Meigle** P & K
16 C3 **Melbourn** Cambs
29 K7 **Melbourne** Derbys
27 J2 **Meliden** Denbgs
13 J5 **Melksham** Wilts
37 J6 **Melling** Lancs
42 F6 **Melmerby** Cumb
33 K5 **Meltham** Kirk
34 F4 **Melton** E R Yk
25 H3 **Melton Constable** Norfk
30 D7 **Melton Mowbray** Leics
57 G2 **Melvaig** Highld
64 E2 **Melvich** Highld
61 G3 **Memsie** Abers
51 J2 **Memus** Angus
26 E3 **Menai Bridge** IoA
14 F7 **Mentmore** Bucks
13 H7 **Mere** Wilts
22 D3 **Meriden** Solhll
12 B2 **Merthyr Tydfil** Myr Td
4 E6 **Merton** Devon
34 F6 **Messingham** N Linc
25 K7 **Metfield** Suffk
51 J6 **Methil** Fife
60 F5 **Methlick** Abers
50 F4 **Methven** P & K
24 E6 **Methwold** Norfk
2 F6 **Mevagissey** Cnwll
34 B6 **Mexborough** Donc
62 f3 **Miabhig** W Isls
62 f3 **Miavaig** W Isls
8 F2 **Micheldever** Hants
37 M2 **Mickleton** Dur
22 C6 **Mickleton** Gloucs
65 c2 **Midbea** Ork
38 B4 **Middleham** N York
35 G7 **Middle Rasen** Lincs
38 E2 **Middlesbrough** Middsb
22 F6 **Middleton Cheney** Nhants
37 M2 **Middleton-in-Teesdale** Dur
9 J5 **Middleton-on-Sea** W Susx
34 F2 **Middleton on the Wolds** E R Yk
14 C2 **Middleton Stoney** Oxon
2 a2 **Middle Town** IoS
8 D3 **Middle Wallop** Hants
28 E3 **Middlewich** Ches E
12 E7 **Middlezoy** Somset
9 J4 **Midhurst** W Susx
13 G6 **Midsomer Norton** BaNES
61 d2 **Mid Yell** Shet
7 J1 **Milborne Port** Somset
24 E7 **Mildenhall** Suffk
47 J6 **Milfield** Nthumb
18 C5 **Milford Haven** Pembks
8 D6 **Milford on Sea** Hants
3 K5 **Millbrook** Cnwll
7 b2 **Millbrook** Jersey
36 E5 **Millom** Cumb

44 F3 **Millport** N Ayrs
50 F6 **Milnathort** P & K
45 J1 **Milngavie** E Duns
7 K2 **Milton Abbas** Dorset
3 K3 **Milton Abbot** Devon
4 D6 **Milton Damerel** Devon
23 K5 **Milton Ernest** Bed
5 K5 **Milton Keynes** M Keyn
5 K5 **Milverton** Somset
13 J2 **Minchinhampton** Gloucs
5 J3 **Minehead** Somset
11 H2 **Minster** Kent
11 L2 **Minster** Kent
28 B8 **Minsterley** Shrops
14 A3 **Minster Lovell** Oxon
61 G4 **Mintlaw** Abers
33 K5 **Mirfield** Kirk
34 E7 **Misterton** Notts
7 H2 **Misterton** Somset
21 K7 **Mitcheldean** Gloucs
28 E2 **Mobberley** Ches E
40 E6 **Mochrum** D & G
3 M5 **Modbury** Devon
41 L2 **Moffat** D & G
27 K4 **Mold** Flints
41 H3 **Moniaive** D & G
51 K4 **Monifieth** Angus
4 D5 **Monkleigh** Devon
45 G5 **Monkton** S Ayrs
21 J8 **Monmouth** Mons
7 H1 **Montacute** Somset
28 B7 **Montford Bridge** Shrops
20 F1 **Montgomery** Powys
6 a2 **Mont Saint** Guern
29 J2 **Monyash** Derbys
55 K3 **Monymusk** Abers
5 G6 **Morchard Bishop** Devon
23 J1 **Morcott** Rutlnd
21 J6 **Mordiford** Herefs
47 H7 **Morebattle** Border
37 G6 **Morecambe** Lancs
7 K3 **Moreton** Dorset
6 B3 **Moretonhampstead** Devon
22 C6 **Moreton-in-Marsh** Gloucs
26 B5 **Morfa Nefyn** Gwynd
33 L4 **Morley** Leeds
43 J3 **Morpeth** Nthumb
5 G6 **Morston** Norfk
4 D3 **Mortehoe** Devon
14 D7 **Mortimer** W Berk
21 K2 **Morville** Shrops
55 H3 **Mossat** Abers
59 L4 **Mosstodloch** Moray
7 H2 **Mosterton** Dorset
45 K3 **Mostyn** Flints
37 G1 **Motherby** Cumb
45 K3 **Motherwell** N Lans
14 D5 **Moulsford** Oxon
23 H4 **Moulton** Nhants
12 B2 **Mountain Ash** Rhondd
30 C7 **Mountsorrel** Leics
2 B7 **Mousehole** Cnwll
58 F5 **Moy** Highld
55 M5 **Muchalls** Abers
21 J7 **Much Birch** Herefs
16 C5 **Much Hadham** Herts
21 K1 **Much Marcle** Herefs
21 K1 **Much Wenlock** Shrops
4 E4 **Muddiford** Devon
51 K3 **Muirdrum** Angus
51 H4 **Muirhead** Angus
45 K5 **Muirkirk** E Ayrs
58 F4 **Muir of Ord** Highld
37 L4 **Muker** N York
2 D8 **Mullion** Cnwll
25 K3 **Mundesley** Norfk
24 E6 **Mundford** Norfk
42 B8 **Mungrisdale** Cumb
13 H2 **Munlochy** Highld
21 J2 **Munslow** Shrops
46 D3 **Musselburgh** E Loth
50 D5 **Muthill** P & K

N

17 K4 **Nacton** Suffk
12 F4 **Nailsea** N Som
52 F1 **Nailsworth** Gloucs
59 G4 **Nairn** Highld
19 H4 **Nantgaredig** Carmth

28 D5 **Nantwich** Ches E
18 E5 **Narberth** Pembks
24 E4 **Narborough** Norfk
23 G3 **Naseby** Nhants
30 F4 **Navenby** Lincs
17 H4 **Nayland** Suffk
16 C6 **Nazeing** Essex
19 K6 **Neath** Neath
24 F5 **Necton** Norfk
17 J2 **Needham Market** Suffk
26 C5 **Nefyn** Gwynd
33 H3 **Nelson** Lancs
28 B7 **Nesscliffe** Shrops
27 L3 **Neston** Ches W
12 C7 **Nether Stowey** Somset
36 E3 **Nether Wasdale** Cumb
54 D3 **Nethy Bridge** Highld
14 E5 **Nettlebed** Oxon
18 E3 **Nevern** Pembks
41 K5 **New Abbey** D & G
60 F3 **New Aberdour** Abers
8 F3 **New Alresford** Hants
30 E4 **Newark-on-Trent** Notts
45 L2 **Newarthill** N Lans
37 L1 **Newbiggin** Dur
38 A5 **Newbiggin** N York
43 K3 **Newbiggin-by-the-Sea** Nthumb
46 A5 **Newbigging** S Lans
22 D5 **Newbold on Stour** Warwks
31 J4 **New Bolingbroke** Lincs
26 D4 **Newborough** IoA
12 C2 **Newbridge** Caerph
41 K4 **Newbridge** D & G
20 E4 **Newbridge on Wye** Powys
25 H6 **New Buckenham** Norfk
61 G6 **Newburgh** Abers
51 G5 **Newburgh** Fife
14 C6 **Newbury** W Berk
37 G5 **Newby Bridge** Cumb
18 F3 **Newcastle Emlyn** Carmth
42 C3 **Newcastleton** Border
28 F5 **Newcastle-under-Lyme** Staffs
43 K5 **Newcastle upon Tyne** N u Ty
45 J6 **New Cumnock** E Ayrs
60 F5 **New Deer** Abers
21 L7 **Newent** Gloucs
18 C4 **Newgale** Pembks
41 G4 **New Galloway** D & G
2 a1 **New Grimsby** IoS
10 C7 **Newhaven** E Susx
35 G4 **New Holland** N Linc
10 C6 **Newick** E Susx
40 C5 **New Luce** D & G
2 B7 **Newlyn** Cnwll
45 L3 **Newmains** N Lans
16 E2 **Newmarket** Suffk
60 B4 **Newmill** Moray
8 C6 **New Milton** Hants
13 G1 **Newnham** Gloucs
21 K4 **Newnham** Worcs
60 F4 **New Pitsligo** Abers
16 D4 **Newport** Essex
8 E6 **Newport** IoW
12 D3 **Newport** Newpt
18 D3 **Newport** Pembks
28 E7 **Newport** Wrekin
51 J4 **Newport-on-Tay** Fife
23 J6 **Newport Pagnell** M Keyn
19 G1 **New Quay** Cerdgn
2 E5 **Newquay** Cnwll
20 F4 **New Radnor** Powys
11 H5 **New Romney** Kent
38 B3 **Newsham** N York
6 C5 **Newton Abbot** Devon
38 C2 **Newton Aycliffe** Dur
3 L6 **Newton Ferrers** Devon
62 d8 **Newton Ferry** W Isls
46 D4 **Newtongrange** Mdloth
45 J3 **Newton Mearns** E Rens
54 B4 **Newtonmore** Highld
43 J2 **Newton-on-the-Moor** Nthumb
30 E3 **Newton on Trent** Lincs

6 C3 **Newton St Cyres** Devon
29 J7 **Newton Solney** Derbys
40 E5 **Newton Stewart** D & G
21 K5 **Newtown** Herefs
20 F2 **Newtown** Powys
12 C2 **New Tredegar** Caerph
51 H3 **Newtyle** Angus
18 D5 **Neyland** Pembks
59 G3 **Nigg** Highld
10 E6 **Ninfield** E Susx
8 F7 **Niton** IoW
31 G4 **Nocton** Lincs
47 J5 **Norham** Nthumb
34 B4 **Normanton** Wakefd
15 G2 **Northall** Bucks
38 D4 **Northallerton** N York
4 D4 **Northam** Devon
23 H4 **Northampton** Nhants
46 F2 **North Berwick** E Loth
34 F4 **North Cave** E R Yk
9 J3 **Northchapel** W Susx
7 G3 **North Chideock** Dorset
35 K6 **North Cotes** Lincs
24 F3 **North Creake** Norfk
12 D8 **North Curry** Somset
34 F2 **North Dalton** E R Yk
34 B4 **North Elmham** Norfk
35 G4 **North Ferriby** E R Yk
35 H2 **North Frodingham** E R Yk
39 H6 **North Grimston** N York
9 G5 **North Hayling** Hants
30 F3 **North Hykeham** Lincs
11 G6 **Northiam** E Susx
58 F4 **North Kessock** Highld
23 H3 **North Kilworth** Leics
31 H4 **North Kyme** Lincs
22 C8 **Northleach** Gloucs
23 J1 **North Luffenham** Rutlnd
5 G4 **North Molton** Devon
30 E4 **North Muskham** Notts
27 K3 **Northop** Flints
12 D7 **North Petherton** Somset
33 L2 **North Rigton** N York
43 K5 **North Shields** N Tyne
35 K6 **North Somercotes** Lincs
25 J3 **North Walsham** Norfk
8 F2 **North Waltham** Hants
16 D6 **North Weald Bassett** Essex
28 D3 **Northwich** Ches W
29 K4 **North Wingfield** Derbys
24 E6 **Northwold** Norfk
39 G6 **Norton** N York
13 H5 **Norton St Philip** Somset
25 J5 **Norwich** Norfk
30 C5 **Nottingham** C Nott
22 E2 **Nuneaton** Warwks
13 H6 **Nunney** Somset
10 C5 **Nutley** E Susx

O

23 G1 **Oadby** Leics
30 E8 **Oakham** Rutlnd
13 G6 **Oakhill** Somset
23 K5 **Oakley** Bed
14 D3 **Oakley** Bucks
8 F2 **Oakley** Hants
13 L5 **Oare** Wilts
52 F7 **Oban** Ag & B
45 H5 **Ochiltree** E Ayrs
29 L6 **Ockbrook** Derbys
9 G2 **Ockley** Surrey
8 F2 **Odiham** Hants
13 M4 **Offenham** Worcs
13 M4 **Ogbourne St George** Wilts
19 L8 **Ogmore-by-Sea** V Glam
4 E7 **Okehampton** Devon
61 G4 **Old Deer** Abers
2 a1 **Old Grimsby** IoS
29 J6 **Oldham** Oldham
24 A7 **Old Hurst** Cambs
35 K5 **Old Leake** Lincs
60 F6 **Oldmeldrum** Abers
60 D6 **Old Rayne** Abers

13 H3 **Old Sodbury** S Glos
23 H6 **Old Stratford** Nhants
2 b2 **Old Town** IoS
15 G6 **Old Windsor** W & M
61 b3 **Ollaberry** Shet
30 C3 **Ollerton** Notts
23 J5 **Olney** M Keyn
21 M4 **Ombersley** Worcs
36 c3 **Onchan** IoM
53 G5 **Onich** Highld
17 L3 **Orford** Suffk
25 L4 **Ormesby St Margaret** Norfk
32 D6 **Ormskirk** Lancs
10 D2 **Orpington** Gt Lon
10 E1 **Orsett** Thurr
37 J3 **Orton** Cumb
31 G6 **Osbournby** Lincs
7 K4 **Osmington** Dorset
38 E4 **Osmotherley** N York
11 H3 **Ospringe** Kent
33 L5 **Ossett** Wakefd
38 F5 **Oswaldkirk** N York
27 L6 **Oswestry** Shrops
10 D3 **Otford** Kent
12 E7 **Othery** Somset
33 K3 **Otley** Leeds
8 E4 **Otterbourne** Hants
43 G3 **Otterburn** Nthumb
49 H5 **Otter Ferry** Ag & B
15 G7 **Ottershaw** Surrey
6 E4 **Otterton** Devon
6 E3 **Ottery St Mary** Devon
23 K2 **Oundle** Nhants
24 C5 **Outwell** Norfk
29 K7 **Overseal** Derbys
8 F2 **Overton** Hants
28 B5 **Overton** Wrexhm
8 D4 **Ower** Hants
14 C3 **Oxford** Oxon
10 C3 **Oxted** Surrey
30 C5 **Oxton** Notts
19 H7 **Oxwich** Swans

P

23 H7 **Padbury** Bucks
10 E4 **Paddock Wood** Kent
33 G4 **Padiham** Lancs
2 F4 **Padstow** Cnwll
6 C5 **Paignton** Torbay
22 F3 **Pailton** Warwks
13 J1 **Painswick** Gloucs
45 H2 **Paisley** Rens
41 J6 **Palnackie** D & G
21 G7 **Pandy** Mons
14 D6 **Pangbourne** W Berk
33 L2 **Pannal** N York
20 E3 **Pant-y-dwr** Powys
16 B2 **Papworth Everard** Cambs
4 F3 **Parracombe** Devon
38 B6 **Pateley Bridge** N York
45 H6 **Patna** E Ayrs
36 b3 **Patrick** IoM
35 J4 **Patrington** E R Yk
37 G2 **Patterdale** Cumb
23 H7 **Pattishall** Nhants
10 C7 **Peacehaven** E Susx
13 H5 **Peasedown St John** BaNES
11 G6 **Peasmarsh** E Susx
46 C5 **Peebles** Border
36 b3 **Peel** IoM
3 H5 **Pelynt** Cnwll
19 G6 **Pembrey** Carmth
21 H4 **Pembridge** Herefs
18 D6 **Pembroke** Pembks
18 D6 **Pembroke Dock** Pembks
10 E4 **Pembury** Kent
18 E6 **Penally** Pembks
12 C4 **Penarth** V Glam
12 A3 **Pencoed** Brdgnd
21 J7 **Pencraig** Herefs
18 F5 **Pendine** Carmth
21 L6 **Pendock** Worcs
3 G3 **Pendoggett** Cnwll
12 C2 **Pengam** Caerph
46 C4 **Penicuik** Mdloth
33 L6 **Penistone** Barns
29 G7 **Penkridge** Staffs
27 G5 **Penmachno** Conwy
26 F3 **Penmaenmawr** Conwy
20 B1 **Pennal** Gwynd
60 F3 **Pennan** Abers
41 J3 **Penpont** D & G

26 E6 **Penrhyndeudraeth** Gwynd
42 D8 **Penrith** Cumb
2 E7 **Penryn** Cnwll
13 G5 **Pensford** BaNES
10 D4 **Penshurst** Kent
3 J4 **Pensilva** Cnwll
2 F6 **Pentewan** Cnwll
26 D3 **Pentraeth** IoA
27 G5 **Pentrefoelas** Conwy
20 F4 **Penybont** Powys
27 J7 **Pen-y-bont-fawr** Powys
26 D4 **Penygroes** Gwynd
2 B7 **Penzance** Cnwll
2 D5 **Perranporth** Cnwll
22 A5 **Pershore** Worcs
50 F4 **Perth** P & K
23 M1 **Peterborough** C Pete
21 H6 **Peterchurch** Herefs
55 L4 **Peterculter** C Aber
61 H5 **Peterhead** Abers
43 L7 **Peterlee** Dur
9 H4 **Petersfield** Hants
5 J5 **Petton** Devon
9 J4 **Petworth** W Susx
10 E7 **Pevensey** E Susx
13 L5 **Pewsey** Wilts
39 G5 **Pickering** N York
38 C2 **Piercebridge** Darltn
65 c1 **Pierowall** Ork
3 J4 **Pillaton** Cnwll
22 D5 **Pillerton Priors** Warwks
32 D3 **Pilling** Lancs
31 H7 **Pinchbeck** Lincs
40 C3 **Pinwherry** S Ayrs
29 L4 **Pinxton** Derbys
15 G7 **Pirbright** Surrey
60 E6 **Pitcaple** Abers
50 E2 **Pitlochry** P & K
60 F6 **Pitmedden** Abers
51 K6 **Pittenweem** Fife
30 B4 **Pleasley** Derbys
57 H6 **Plockton** Highld
11 G4 **Pluckley** Kent
10 C6 **Plumpton** E Susx
30 C6 **Plumtree** Notts
3 K5 **Plymouth** C Plym
3 L5 **Plympton** C Plym
34 E2 **Pocklington** E R Yk
3 J5 **Polbathic** Cnwll
10 D7 **Polegate** E Susx
50 E8 **Polmont** Falk
3 H5 **Polperro** Cnwll
3 G5 **Polruan** Cnwll
2 F3 **Polzeath** Cnwll
19 K6 **Pontardawe** Neath
19 J6 **Pontarddulais** Swans
34 B5 **Pontefract** Wakefd
43 J4 **Ponteland** Nthumb
20 C3 **Ponterwyd** Cerdgn
28 B8 **Pontesbury** Shrops
12 C2 **Pontllanfraith** Caerph
19 K1 **Pontrhydfendigaid** Cerdgn
21 H7 **Pontrilas** Herefs
19 H5 **Pontyates** Carmth
19 H5 **Pontyberem** Carmth
12 D2 **Pontypool** Torfn
12 B3 **Pontypridd** Rhondd
33 L3 **Pool** Leeds
8 A7 **Poole** Poole
57 H2 **Poolewe** Highld
37 H2 **Pooley Bridge** Cumb
5 H3 **Porlock** Somset
5 H3 **Porlock Weir** Somset
52 F6 **Port Appin** Ag & B
49 H6 **Port Askaig** Ag & B
49 H6 **Portavadie** Ag & B
49 J6 **Port Bannatyne** Ag & B
42 A5 **Port Carlisle** Cumb
48 B7 **Port Charlotte** Ag & B
9 J5 **Portchester** Hants
19 H7 **Port Einon** Swans
49 H5 **Port Ellen** Ag & B
36 a4 **Port Erin** IoM
7 J3 **Portesham** Dorset
49 L5 **Port Glasgow** Inver
60 B2 **Portgordon** Moray
12 B3 **Porth** Rhondd
19 L8 **Porthcawl** Brdgnd
2 E4 **Porthcothan** Cnwll
2 A8 **Porthcurno** Cnwll
57 G3 **Port Henderson** Highld
2 C7 **Porthleven** Cnwll
26 E6 **Porthmadog** Gwynd
2 D6 **Porthtowan** Cnwll

36 F2 **Portinscale** Cumb
2 F3 **Port Isaac** Cnwll
12 F4 **Portishead** N Som
60 C3 **Portknockie** Moray
55 M5 **Portlethen** Abers
2 F6 **Portloe** Cnwll
40 C7 **Port Logan** D & G
59 H2 **Portmahomack** Highld
53 G6 **Portnacroish** Ag & B
48 A7 **Portnahaven** Ag & B
62 d8 **Port nan Long** W Isls
62 i1 **Port Nis** W Isls
50 B6 **Port of Menteith** Stirlg
62 i1 **Port of Ness** W Isls
40 B6 **Portpatrick** D & G
2 C6 **Portreath** Cnwll
56 E5 **Portree** Highld
36 a4 **Port St Mary** IoM
2 E7 **Portscatho** Cnwll
64 E2 **Portskerra** Highld
10 B7 **Portslade-by-Sea** Br & H
9 G5 **Portsmouth** C Port
60 D3 **Portsoy** Abers
19 K7 **Port Talbot** Neath
40 E7 **Port William** D & G
3 M3 **Postbridge** Devon
14 E4 **Postcombe** Oxon
13 K5 **Potterne** Wilts
15 J4 **Potters Bar** Herts
16 B3 **Potton** C Beds
32 C3 **Poulton-le-Fylde** Lancs
47 K7 **Powburn** Nthumb
21 M5 **Powick** Worcs
28 F2 **Poynton** Ches E
2 C7 **Praa Sands** Cnwll
28 C6 **Prees** Shrops
32 D3 **Preesall** Lancs
28 C6 **Prees Green** Shrops
26 E5 **Prenteg** Gwynd
27 J2 **Prestatyn** Denbgs
28 F3 **Prestbury** Ches E
21 G4 **Presteigne** Powys
47 H4 **Preston** Border
32 E4 **Preston** Lancs
8 F2 **Preston Candover** Hants
22 F5 **Preston Capes** Nhants
46 E3 **Prestonpans** E Loth
33 G6 **Prestwich** Bury
45 G5 **Prestwick** S Ayrs
12 F6 **Priddy** Somset
14 F4 **Princes Risborough** Bucks
22 E3 **Princethorpe** Warwks
3 L4 **Princetown** Devon
41 L7 **Prospect** Cumb
43 H5 **Prudhoe** Nthumb
13 H4 **Pucklechurch** S Glos
7 K3 **Puddletown** Dorset
33 L4 **Pudsey** Leeds
9 K4 **Pulborough** W Susx
28 B4 **Pulford** Ches W
25 J7 **Pulham St Mary** Norfk
19 J3 **Pumsaint** Carmth
10 D1 **Purfleet** Thurr
13 L3 **Purton** Wilts
19 H6 **Pwll** Carmth
26 C6 **Pwllheli** Gwynd
10 B6 **Pyecombe** W Susx
19 L7 **Pyle** Brdgnd

Q

21 L2 **Quatt** Shrops
27 L3 **Queensferry** Flints
16 D4 **Quendon** Essex

R

5 H5 **Rackenford** Devon
25 J4 **Rackheath** Norfk
30 C6 **Radcliffe on Trent** Notts
15 H4 **Radlett** Herts
13 G5 **Radstock** BaNES
16 E4 **Radwinter** Essex
12 C4 **Radyr** Cardif
59 J4 **Rafford** Moray
12 E1 **Raglan** Mons
10 D1 **Rainham** Gt Lon
36 F6 **Rampside** Cumb
14 A6 **Ramsbury** Wilts

24 A7 **Ramsey** Cambs
36 c2 **Ramsey** IoM
11 L2 **Ramsgate** Kent
53 L5 **Rannoch Station** P & K
65 c2 **Rapness** Ork
61 G3 **Rathen** Abers
23 K3 **Raunds** Nhants
39 J3 **Ravenglass** Cumb
39 J3 **Ravenscar** N York
37 K3 **Ravenstonedale** Cumb
34 B7 **Rawmarsh** Rothm
33 G4 **Rawtenstall** Lancs
16 F7 **Rayleigh** Essex
14 E6 **Reading** Readg
64 F2 **Reay** Highld
11 K2 **Reculver** Kent
15 H3 **Redbourn** Herts
12 F1 **Redbrook** Gloucs
28 C5 **Redbrook** Wrexhm
38 F2 **Redcar** R & Cl
22 B4 **Redditch** Worcs
25 G7 **Redgrave** Suffk
12 F5 **Redhill** N Som
10 B4 **Redhill** Surrey
30 E6 **Redmile** Leics
28 B6 **Rednal** Shrops
18 F5 **Red Roses** Carmth
43 K2 **Red Row** Nthumb
2 D6 **Redruth** Cnwll
26 D2 **Red Wharf Bay** IoA
25 H4 **Reedham** Norfk
25 H4 **Reepham** Norfk
10 B4 **Reigate** Surrey
39 K5 **Reighton** N York
18 D5 **Rempstone** Notts
45 H2 **Renfrew** Rens
42 D7 **Renwick** Cumb
29 K6 **Repton** Derbys
19 L6 **Resolven** Neath
30 D2 **Retford** Notts
19 H7 **Reynoldston** Swans
20 D4 **Rhayader** Powys
63 H3 **Rhiconich** Highld
5 J2 **Rhoose** V Glam
27 L5 **Rhoslanerchrugog** Wrexhm
26 C3 **Rhosneigr** IoA
19 G7 **Rhôs-on-Sea** Conwy
19 G7 **Rhossili** Swans
49 L5 **Rhu** Ag & B
27 J3 **Rhuddlan** Denbgs
26 E4 **Rhyd-Ddu** Gwynd
19 G2 **Rhydowen** Cerdgn
27 J2 **Rhyl** Denbgs
12 C1 **Rhymney** Caerph
21 J4 **Richards Castle** Herefs
15 J6 **Richmond** Gt Lon
38 B3 **Richmond** N York
15 H4 **Rickmansworth** Herts
43 G4 **Ridsdale** Nthumb
39 H5 **Rillington** N York
41 G6 **Ringford** D & G
10 C6 **Ringmer** E Susx
8 C5 **Ringwood** Hants
29 K5 **Ripley** Derbys
38 C7 **Ripley** N York
15 H7 **Ripley** Surrey
38 D6 **Ripon** N York
21 M6 **Ripple** Worcs
33 J5 **Ripponden** Calder
12 B3 **Risca** Caerph
31 H6 **Risegate** Lincs
14 E7 **Riseley** Bed
29 L6 **Risley** Derbys
32 F7 **Risley** Warrtn
23 H5 **Roade** Nhants
46 E7 **Roberton** Border
45 M5 **Roberton** S Lans
10 F6 **Robertsbridge** E Susx
18 E5 **Roberton Wathen** Pembks
39 J3 **Robin Hood's Bay** N York
29 H6 **Rocester** Staffs
18 C4 **Roch** Pembks
33 H5 **Rochdale** Rochdl
2 F5 **Roche** Cnwll
10 F2 **Rochester** Medway
42 F3 **Rochester** Nthumb
17 G2 **Rochford** Essex
2 F3 **Rock** Cnwll
42 B5 **Rockcliffe** Cumb
41 J6 **Rockcliffe** D & G
23 J2 **Rockingham** Nhants
9 H4 **Rogate** W Susx
12 D3 **Rogerstone** Newpt

25 L4 **Rollesby** Norfk
11 G5 **Rolvenden** Kent
37 M2 **Romaldkirk** Dur
46 C7 **Romanno Bridge** Border
16 D7 **Romford** Gt Lon
8 D4 **Romsey** Hants
43 G7 **Rookhope** Dur
9 G3 **Ropley** Hants
39 G4 **Rosedale Abbey** N York
63 K7 **Rosehall** Highld
61 G3 **Rosehearty** Abers
58 F4 **Rosemarkie** Highld
28 B4 **Rosewell** Mdloth
21 K7 **Ross-on-Wye** Herefs
46 B2 **Rosyth** Fife
43 H2 **Rothbury** Nthumb
10 D5 **Rotherfield** E Susx
34 B7 **Rotherham** Rothm
59 L4 **Rothes** Moray
49 J6 **Rothesay** Ag & B
33 M4 **Rothwell** Leeds
23 H3 **Rothwell** Nhants
10 C7 **Rottingdean** Br & H
25 J3 **Roughton** Norfk
9 G5 **Rowland's Castle** Hants
43 J6 **Rowland's Gill** Gatesd
29 J3 **Rowsley** Derbys
47 G6 **Roxburgh** Border
16 E6 **Roxwell** Essex
34 A5 **Royston** Barns
16 C4 **Royston** Herts
7 C1 **Rozel** Jersey
27 L5 **Ruabon** Wrexhm
30 C6 **Ruddington** Notts
9 K3 **Rudgwick** W Susx
39 K6 **Rudston** E R Yk
32 D5 **Rufford** Lancs
22 F3 **Rugby** Warwks
29 G7 **Rugeley** Staffs
50 F6 **Rumbling Bridge** P & K
28 C2 **Runcorn** Halton
23 K4 **Rushden** Nhants
38 C1 **Rushyford** Dur
31 G5 **Ruskington** Lincs
9 K5 **Rustington** W Susx
39 H3 **Ruswarp** N York
45 J2 **Rutherglen** S Lans
27 J4 **Ruthin** Denbgs
28 B7 **Ruyton-XI-Towns** Shrops
37 G3 **Rydal** Cumb
8 F6 **Ryde** IoW
11 G6 **Rye** E Susx

S

44 B5 **Saddell** Ag & B
16 D4 **Saffron Walden** Essex
47 J3 **St Abbs** Border
2 D5 **St Agnes** Cnwll
15 H3 **St Albans** Herts
6 a2 **St Andrew** Guern
51 K5 **St Andrews** Fife
12 F2 **St Arvans** Mons
27 J3 **St Asaph** Denbgs
5 J1 **St Athan** V Glam
7 b2 **St Aubin** Jersey
2 F5 **St Austell** Cnwll
36 D3 **St Bees** Cumb
3 G5 **St Blazey** Cnwll
46 F6 **St Boswells** Border
7 a2 **St Brelade** Jersey
7 a2 **St Brelade's Bay** Jersey
12 F2 **St Briavels** Gloucs
2 A7 **St Buryan** Cnwll
49 J3 **St Catherines** Ag & B
18 F5 **St Clears** Carmth
3 H4 **St Cleer** Cnwll
7 c2 **St Clement** Jersey
2 F4 **St Columb Major** Cnwll
61 H3 **St Combs** Abers
55 K7 **St Cyrus** Abers
18 B4 **St David's** Pembks
2 D6 **St Day** Cnwll
18 E2 **St Dogmaels** Pembks
61 H4 **St Fergus** Abers
50 C4 **St Fillans** P & K
18 E6 **St Florence** Pembks
8 F6 **St Helens** IoW
32 E7 **St Helens** St Hel

7 b2 **St Helier** Jersey
24 A8 **St Ives** Cambs
2 B6 **St Ives** Cnwll
7 b1 **St John** Jersey
36 b3 **St John's** IoM
43 G7 **St John's Chapel** Dur
41 G4 **St John's Town of Dalry** D & G
36 c2 **St Jude's** IoM
2 A7 **St Just** Cnwll
2 E7 **St Just-in-Roseland** Cnwll
2 E8 **St Keverne** Cnwll
3 H5 **St Keyne** Cnwll
8 F7 **St Lawrence** IoW
7 b1 **St Lawrence** Jersey
11 L4 **St Margaret's at Cliffe** Kent
65 c5 **St Margaret's Hope** Ork
36 b3 **St Marks** IoM
6 b2 **St Martin** Guern
7 c1 **St Martin** Jersey
7 b1 **St Mary** Jersey
65 c4 **St Mary's** Ork
1 J5 **St Mary's Bay** Kent
2 E7 **St Mawes** Cnwll
2 E4 **St Mawgan** Cnwll
51 K6 **St Monans** Fife
23 M4 **St Neots** Cambs
17 J5 **St Osyth** Essex
7 a1 **St Ouen** Jersey
21 J7 **St Owens Cross** Herefs
7 b1 **St Peter** Jersey
6 b2 **St Peter Port** Guern
6 a2 **St Peter's** Guern
6 b1 **St Sampson** Guern
6 a2 **St Saviour** Guern
7 b2 **St Saviour** Jersey
2 F5 **St Stephen** Cnwll
3 G3 **St Tudy** Cnwll
6 B7 **Salcombe** Devon
33 G7 **Sale** Traffd
52 D6 **Salen** Ag & B
52 E4 **Salen** Highld
10 B4 **Salfords** Surrey
50 F7 **Saline** Fife
13 K5 **Salisbury** Wilts
3 K5 **Saltash** Cnwll
38 F2 **Saltburn-by-the-Sea** R & Cl
44 F4 **Saltcoats** N Ayrs
35 K7 **Saltfleet** Lincs
5 K5 **Sampford Arundel** Somset
5 J3 **Sampford Brett** Somset
48 B6 **Sanaigmore** Ag & B
28 E4 **Sandbach** Ches E
49 K5 **Sandbank** Ag & B
14 C4 **Sandford-on-Thames** Oxon
61 G3 **Sandhaven** Abers
40 C6 **Sandhead** D & G
14 F7 **Sandhurst** Br For
61 a5 **Sandness** Shet
29 G6 **Sandon** Staffs
8 F7 **Sandown** IoW
15 J3 **Sandridge** Herts
39 H3 **Sandsend** N York
11 L3 **Sandwich** Kent
61 c7 **Sandwick** Shet
23 L5 **Sandy** C Beds
45 L6 **Sanquhar** D & G
26 B6 **Sarn** Gwynd
11 K2 **Sarre** Kent
34 E7 **Saundby** Notts
18 E5 **Saundersfoot** Pembks
4 D4 **Saunton** Devon
16 D5 **Sawbridgeworth** Herts
16 D3 **Sawston** Cambs
23 L2 **Sawtry** Cambs
30 E2 **Saxby** Leics
30 E3 **Saxilby** Lincs
17 L2 **Saxmundham** Suffk
25 H3 **Saxthorpe** Norfk
48 C4 **Scalasaig** Ag & B
39 J2 **Scalby** N York
61 c6 **Scalloway** Shet
31 J3 **Scamblesby** Lincs
39 K4 **Scarborough** N York
48 b2 **Scarinish** Ag & B
34 F6 **Scawby** N Linc
25 H7 **Scole** Norfk
51 G4 **Scone** P & K
56 E6 **Sconser** Highld
38 C3 **Scotch Corner** N York
34 F6 **Scotter** Lincs
38 B4 **Scotton** N York

25 G5	Scoulton Norfk	37 H5	Silverdale Lancs
63 G4	Scourie Highld	16 F5	Silver End Essex
65 G2	Scrabster Highld	23 G6	Silverstone Nhants
34 F5	Scunthorpe N Linc	5 H6	Silverton Devon
10 D7	Seaford E Susx	42 F4	Simonburn Nthumb
43 L6	Seaham Dur	5 G4	Simonsbath Somset
47 L6	Seahouses Nthumb	9 J4	Singleton W Susx
10 D3	Seal Kent	10 F4	Sissinghurst Kent
39 J5	Seamer N York	11 G3	Sittingbourne Kent
25 L3	Sea Palling Norfk	8 A4	Sixpenny Handley Dorset
36 D3	Seascale Cumb		
36 F4	Seathwaite Cumb	31 L4	Skegness Lincs
6 F3	Seaton Devon	30 F3	Skellingthorpe Lincs
43 K4	Seaton Delaval Nthumb	32 D6	Skelmersdale Lancs
		49 K6	Skelmorlie N Ayrs
38 F4	Seave Green N York	42 C7	Skelton Cumb
9 G6	Seaview IoW	38 F2	Skelton R & Cl
37 J4	Sedbergh Cumb	21 H7	Skenfrith Mons
22 B6	Sedgeberrow Worcs	64 C2	Skerray Highld
30 E6	Sedgebrook Lincs	44 C3	Skipness Ag & B
38 D1	Sedgefield Dur	35 H2	Skipsea E R Yk
10 F6	Sedlescombe E Susx	33 J2	Skipton N York
13 K5	Seend Wilts	46 B6	Skirling Border
9 G3	Selborne Hants	42 D8	Skirwith Cumb
34 D4	Selby N York	32 F2	Slaidburn Lancs
46 E6	Selkirk Border	43 G6	Slaley Nthumb
11 J4	Sellindge Kent	45 L1	Slamannan Falk
9 H6	Selsey W Susx	6 B7	Slapton Devon
29 L4	Selston Notts	31 G5	Sleaford Lincs
15 G7	Send Surrey	39 J6	Sledmere E R Yk
2 A7	Sennen Cnwll	39 H3	Sleights N York
20 D7	Sennybridge Powys	39 G5	Slingsby N York
24 D4	Setchey Norfk	15 G5	Slough Slough
37 L6	Settle N York	47 G6	Smailholm Border
10 D3	Sevenoaks Kent	11 G4	Smarden Kent
19 L5	Seven Sisters Neath	42 C5	Smithfield Cumb
13 J8	Shaftesbury Dorset	39 J5	Snainton N York
16 F4	Shalford Essex	17 L2	Snape Suffk
9 K2	Shalford Surrey	24 E3	Snettisham Norfk
49 K5	Shandon Ag & B	10 E3	Snodland Kent
8 F7	Shanklin IoW	24 D7	Soham Cambs
37 H2	Shap Cumb	22 C3	Solihull Solhll
29 L6	Shardlow Derbys	18 B4	Solva Pembks
23 K4	Sharnbrook Bed	24 B7	Somersham Cambs
13 G2	Sharpness Gloucs	12 F7	Somerton Somset
3 L4	Shaugh Prior Devon	9 L5	Sompting W Susx
28 E5	Shavington Ches E	14 E6	Sonning Wokham
28 C7	Shawbury Shrops	14 E5	Sonning Common Oxon
4 D6	Shebbear Devon		
4 E6	Sheepwash Devon	40 E6	Sorbie D & G
11 G2	Sheerness Kent	37 K3	Soulby Cumb
29 K2	Sheffield Sheff	22 F6	Souldern Oxon
23 L6	Shefford C Beds	23 K4	Souldrop Bed
16 C3	Shepreth Cambs	3 L2	Sourton Devon
30 B7	Shepshed Leics	22 E4	Southam Warwks
13 G6	Shepton Mallet Somset	8 E5	Southampton C Sotn
		16 F8	South Benfleet Essex
7 J1	Sherborne Dorset	10 D4	Southborough Kent
39 J5	Sherburn N York	6 A5	South Brent Devon
34 C4	Sherburn in Elmet N York	34 F4	South Cave E R Yk
		34 B5	South Elmsall Wakefd
14 D7	Sherfield on Loddon Hants	44 B6	Southend Ag & B
		17 G8	Southend-on-Sea Sthend
38 F6	Sheriff Hutton N York		
25 H2	Sheringham Norfk	24 D6	Southery Norfk
57 J7	Shiel Bridge Highld	9 H4	South Harting W Susx
57 H4	Shieldaig Highld	9 G5	South Hayling Hants
28 E8	Shifnal Shrops	9 L2	South Holmwood Surrey
38 C2	Shildon Dur		
14 D4	Shillingford Oxon	31 H5	South Kyme Lincs
7 L2	Shillingstone Dorset	15 J4	South Mimms Herts
14 E6	Shinfield Wokham	17 H7	Southminster Essex
63 K6	Shinness Highld	4 F5	South Molton Devon
25 G5	Shipdham Norfk	14 B4	Southmoor Oxon
14 E6	Shiplake Oxon	29 L4	South Normanton Derbys
33 K3	Shipley C Brad		
22 D6	Shipston on Stour Warwks	16 E8	South Ockendon Thurr
		7 G1	South Petherton Somset
38 E7	Shipton N York		
34 E3	Shiptonthorpe E R Yk	32 B6	Southport Sefton
30 B3	Shirebrook Derbys	46 B3	South Queensferry C Edin
9 L5	Shoreham-by-Sea W Susx		
		24 F4	South Raynham Norfk
8 E7	Shorwell IoW	25 J3	Southrepps Norfk
17 K4	Shotley Suffk	9 G6	Southsea C Port
17 L3	Shottisham Suffk	43 L5	South Shields S Tyne
45 L2	Shotts N Lans	38 C6	South Stainley N York
28 C8	Shrewsbury Shrops	25 K4	South Walsham Norfk
13 L6	Shrewton Wilts	30 D4	Southwell Notts
13 M3	Shrivenham Oxon	9 G5	Southwick Hants
22 A7	Shurdington Gloucs	9 L5	Southwick W Susx
6 F3	Shute Devon	30 F7	South Witham Lincs
31 J5	Sibsey Lincs	25 L3	Southwold Suffk
22 E1	Sibson Leics	16 F7	South Woodham Ferrers Essex
6 E3	Sidmouth Devon		
14 D7	Silchester Hants	3 M2	South Zeal Devon
30 C7	Sileby Leics	38 D5	Sowerby N York
13 G5	Silk Willoughby Lincs	33 J4	Sowerby Bridge Calder
41 L6	Silloth Cumb		
23 L6	Silsoe C Beds		
31 H7	Spalding Lincs	28 F6	Stone Staffs
13 G8	Sparkford Somset	55 L5	Stonehaven Abers
8 E3	Sparsholt Hants	13 H2	Stonehouse Gloucs
53 J3	Spean Bridge Highld	45 K3	Stonehouse S Lans
43 K7	Spennymoor Dur	40 B6	Stoneykirk D & G
7 L2	Spetisbury Dorset	14 E5	Stonor Oxon
60 B3	Spey Bay Moray	62 h3	Stornoway W Isls
31 K3	Spilsby Lincs	9 K4	Storrington W Susx
58 F1	Spinningdale Highld	16 A4	Stotfold C Beds
65 H3	Spittal Highld	22 A5	Stoulton Worcs
54 E7	Spittal of Glenshee P & K	21 M3	Stourbridge Dudley
		7 L2	Stourpaine Dorset
25 J4	Spixworth Norfk	21 L3	Stourport-on-Severn Worcs
34 A2	Spofforth N York		
41 H5	Springholm D & G	21 M2	Stourton Staffs
35 H4	Sproatley E R Yk	46 E5	Stow Border
14 D4	Stadhampton Oxon	16 D2	Stow-cum-Quy Cambs
62 c11	Stadhlaigearraidh W Isls	17 H2	Stowmarket Suffk
		22 C7	Stow-on-the-Wold Gloucs
56 E3	Staffin Highld		
28 F7	Stafford Staffs	55 K5	Strachan Abers
38 B2	Staindrop Dur	49 J3	Strachur Ag & B
15 G6	Staines Surrey	25 J7	Stradbroke Suffk
37 L6	Stainforth N York	16 F3	Stradishall Suffk
39 G2	Staithes N York	24 D5	Stradsett Norfk
25 K4	Stalham Norfk	45 G7	Straiton S Ayrs
31 G8	Stamford Lincs	40 B5	Stranraer D & G
39 G7	Stamford Bridge E R Yk	14 E7	Stratfield Turgis Hants
		17 L2	Stratford St Andrew Suffk
43 H5	Stamfordham Nthumb		
		22 C5	Stratford-upon-Avon Warwks
41 K7	Standingstone Cumb		
32 E5	Standish Wigan	45 K4	Strathaven S Lans
16 C5	Standon Herts	50 B8	Strathblane Stirlg
14 B4	Stanford in the Vale Oxon	63 G7	Strathcanaird Highld
		55 G3	Strathdon Abers
10 E1	Stanford le Hope Thurr	58 D4	Strathpeffer Highld
		64 E2	Strathy Highld
43 G7	Stanhope Dur	50 B5	Strathyre Stirlg
43 J6	Stanley Dur	4 B6	Stratton Cnwll
50 F4	Stanley P & K	13 G6	Stratton-on-the-Fosse Somset
43 J4	Stannington Nthumb		
16 D5	Stansted Mountfitchet Essex	14 D5	Streatley W Berk
		12 F7	Street Somset
25 G7	Stanton Suffk	38 F7	Strensall C York
13 J4	Stanton St Quintin Wilts	6 C6	Strete Devon
		33 G7	Stretford Traffd
22 B6	Stanway Gloucs	24 C7	Stretham Cambs
6 F1	Staple Fitzpaine Somset	30 F7	Stretton Rutlnd
		55 H5	Strichen Abers
30 B6	Stapleford Notts	57 H5	Stromeferry Highld
10 F4	Staplehurst Kent	65 b4	Stromness Ork
37 M5	Starbotton N York	49 M3	Stronachlachar Stirlg
37 H4	Staveley Cumb	45 K5	Strone Ag & B
29 L3	Staveley Derbys	52 F5	Strontian Highld
22 F4	Staverton Nhants	10 F2	Strood Medway
39 J5	Staxton N York	13 J2	Stroud Gloucs
17 G6	Steeple Essex	58 C5	Struy Highld
22 F6	Steeple Aston Oxon	61 G5	Stuartfield Abers
16 E3	Steeple Bumpstead Essex	8 B7	Studland Dorset
		22 B4	Studley Warwks
50 D8	Stenhousemuir Falk	7 K1	Sturminster Newton Dorset
62 h3	Steornabhagh W Isls		
16 B5	Stevenage Herts	11 J3	Sturry Kent
45 H4	Stevenston N Ayrs	30 E2	Sturton by Stow Lincs
14 C5	Steventon Oxon	29 H6	Sudbury Derbys
45 H3	Stewarton E Ayrs	17 G3	Sudbury Suffk
23 J7	Stewkley Bucks	36 c2	Sulby IoM
9 L5	Steyning W Susx	2 E5	Summercourt Cnwll
4 D5	Stibb Cross Devon	15 H6	Sunbury Surrey
31 J4	Stickford Lincs	43 L6	Sunderland Sundld
31 J4	Stickney Lincs	31 H6	Surfleet Lincs
25 G2	Stiffkey Norfk	31 J6	Sutterton Lincs
62 c11	Stilligarry W Isls	24 C7	Sutton Cambs
38 F6	Stillington N York	10 B2	Sutton Gt Lon
23 L2	Stilton Cambs	13 K4	Sutton Benger Wilts
50 D7	Stirling Stirlg	24 C4	Sutton Bridge Lincs
16 E7	Stock Essex	22 C2	Sutton Coldfield Birm
8 D3	Stockbridge Hants	14 C4	Sutton Courtenay Oxon
33 H7	Stockport Stockp		
33 L6	Stocksbridge Sheff	31 L2	Sutton on Sea Lincs
38 F6	Stockton-on-Tees S on T	38 F6	Sutton-on-the-Forest N York
		30 E3	Sutton on Trent Notts
12 C6	Stogursey Somset	8 E2	Sutton Scotney Hants
16 F3	Stoke by Clare Suffk	10 F4	Sutton Valence Kent
17 H4	Stoke-by-Nayland Suffk	29 K7	Swadlincote Derbys
		24 F5	Swaffham Norfk
6 C6	Stoke Canon Devon	13 H4	Swainswick BaNES
24 E5	Stoke Ferry Norfk	35 H6	Swallow Lincs
6 C6	Stoke Fleming Devon	14 E7	Swallowfield Wokham
6 C6	Stoke Gabriel Devon	8 B7	Swanage Dorset
23 J5	Stoke Goldington M Keyn	10 D2	Swanley Kent
		19 J6	Swansea Swans
21 K5	Stoke Lacy Herefs	29 K4	Swanwick Derbys
14 F3	Stoke Mandeville Bucks	8 F5	Swanwick Hants
		9 L6	Swaton Lincs
14 E4	Stokenchurch Bucks	16 C1	Swavesey Cambs
28 F6	Stoke-on-Trent C Stke		
15 G5	Stoke Poges Bucks	8 D6	Sway Hants
38 E3	Stokesley N York		

13 L3 **Swindon** Swindn
23 K4 **Swineshead** Bed
31 H5 **Swineshead** Lincs
22 F3 **Swinford** Leics
47 H5 **Swinton** Border
34 B6 **Swinton** Rothm
24 F3 **Syderstone** Norfk
61 d4 **Symbister** Shet
45 G5 **Symington** S Ayrs
46 A6 **Symington** S Lans
21 J8 **Symonds Yat** Herefs
23 G6 **Syresham** Nhants
30 C8 **Syston** Leics

T

34 B3 **Tadcaster** N York
14 D7 **Tadley** Hants
59 G2 **Tain** Highld
62 f6 **Tairbeart** W Isls
19 G2 **Talgarreg** Cerdgn
20 F6 **Talgarth** Powys
57 J3 **Talladale** Highld
19 J3 **Talley** Carmth
64 C2 **Talmine** Highld
26 E6 **Talsarnau** Gwynd
20 B2 **Tal-y-bont** Cerdgn
26 F3 **Tal-y-Bont** Conwy
26 E7 **Tal-y-bont** Gwynd
27 G3 **Tal-y-Cafn** Conwy
22 C1 **Tamworth** Staffs
51 J2 **Tannadice** Angus
18 F2 **Tan-y-groes** Cerdgn
14 F5 **Taplow** Bucks
49 G6 **Tarbert** Ag & B
62 f6 **Tarbert** W Isls
49 L3 **Tarbet** Ag & B
45 H5 **Tarbolton** S Ayrs
55 H4 **Tarland** Abers
32 D5 **Tarleton** Lancs
28 C4 **Tarporley** Ches W
7 M2 **Tarrant Hinton** Dorset
56 F7 **Tarskavaig** Highld
60 F6 **Tarves** Abers
28 C3 **Tarvin** Ches W
31 H4 **Tattershall** Lincs
12 D8 **Taunton** Somset
25 H4 **Taverham** Norfk
3 K4 **Tavistock** Devon
44 B3 **Tayinloan** Ag & B
22 D8 **Taynton** Oxon
53 G7 **Taynuilt** Ag & B
51 J4 **Tayport** Fife
48 F5 **Tayvallich** Ag & B
37 J3 **Tebay** Cumb
6 B3 **Tedburn St Mary** Devon
22 A6 **Teddington** Gloucs
6 C4 **Teignmouth** Devon
28 E8 **Telford** Wrekin
46 D4 **Temple** Mdloth
19 H2 **Temple Bar** Cerdgn
13 H8 **Templecombe** Somset
37 J1 **Temple Sowerby** Cumb
23 L5 **Tempsford** C Beds
21 K4 **Tenbury Wells** Worcs
18 E6 **Tenby** Pembks
11 G5 **Tenterden** Kent
28 D6 **Ternhill** Shrops
24 C4 **Terrington St Clement** Norfk
13 J3 **Tetbury** Gloucs
31 J3 **Tetford** Lincs
35 J6 **Tetney** Lincs
14 E4 **Tetsworth** Oxon
42 C2 **Teviothead** Border
21 M6 **Tewkesbury** Gloucs
11 H3 **Teynham** Kent
14 E3 **Thame** Oxon
14 C6 **Thatcham** W Berk
16 E4 **Thaxted** Essex
14 D6 **Theale** W Berk
17 M2 **Theberton** Suffk
36 c2 **The Bungalow** IoM
24 F7 **Thetford** Norfk
16 C7 **Theydon Bois** Essex
38 D5 **Thirsk** N York
13 G3 **Thornbury** S Glos
34 D5 **Thorne** Donc
24 A5 **Thorney** C Pete
24 E2 **Thornham** Norfk
41 J3 **Thornhill** D & G
50 C6 **Thornhill** Stirlg
43 L7 **Thornley** Dur
51 H6 **Thornton** Fife
39 H5 **Thornton le Dale** N York

38 D5 **Thornton-le-Street** N York
38 C5 **Thornton Watlass** N York
25 J5 **Thorpe End** Norfk
17 J5 **Thorpe-le-Soken** Essex
17 M2 **Thorpeness** Suffk
17 J5 **Thorrington** Essex
23 K3 **Thrapston** Nhants
20 F6 **Three Cocks** Powys
31 G6 **Threekingham** Lincs
36 F2 **Threlkeld** Cumb
37 M6 **Threshfield** N York
43 H2 **Thropton** Nthumb
65 J4 **Thrumster** Highld
34 C7 **Thurcroft** Rothm
6 A7 **Thurlestone** Devon
34 B6 **Thurnscoe** Barns
42 B6 **Thursby** Cumb
63 J2 **Thurso** Highld
27 K2 **Thurstaston** Wirral
17 G2 **Thurston** Suffk
37 L4 **Thwaite** N York
14 L4 **Tibshelf** Derbys
10 E5 **Ticehurst** E Susx
34 C7 **Tickhill** Donc
29 K7 **Ticknall** Derbys
29 H3 **Tideswell** Derbys
8 C2 **Tidworth** Wilts
62 c8 **Tigh a Ghearraidh** W Isls
62 c8 **Tigharry** W Isls
10 E2 **Tilbury** Thurr
9 J2 **Tilford** Surrey
50 E6 **Tillicoultry** Clacks
13 K6 **Tilshead** Wilts
28 C6 **Tilstock** Shrops
30 D8 **Tilton on the Hill** Leics
3 G3 **Tintagel** Cnwll
12 F7 **Tintern Parva** Mons
17 G5 **Tiptree** Essex
13 K7 **Tisbury** Wilts
29 J5 **Tissington** Derbys
28 F6 **Tittensor** Staffs
5 H6 **Tiverton** Devon
52 C5 **Tobermory** Ag & B
23 K7 **Toddington** C Beds
33 H4 **Todmorden** Calder
61 c3 **Toft** Shet
38 B1 **Toft Hill** Dur
62 I2 **Tolastadh** W Isls
7 M1 **Tollard Royal** Wilts
17 H6 **Tollesbury** Essex
17 G6 **Tolleshunt D'Arcy** Essex
7 K3 **Tolpuddle** Dorset
62 I2 **Tolsta** W Isls
59 G6 **Tomatin** Highld
54 F3 **Tomintoul** Moray
59 K6 **Tomnavoulin** Moray
10 E4 **Tonbridge** Kent
64 C3 **Tongue** Highld
12 B3 **Tonypandy** Rhondd
12 B3 **Tonyrefail** Rhondd
38 D5 **Topcliffe** N York
6 D3 **Topsham** Devon
44 C5 **Torbeg** N Ayrs
6 B7 **Torcross** Devon
58 E4 **Tore** Highld
30 E3 **Torksey** Lincs
46 A3 **Torphichen** W Loth
55 J4 **Torphins** Abers
3 K5 **Torpoint** Cnwll
6 C5 **Torquay** Torbay
45 J1 **Torrance** E Duns
57 H4 **Torridon** Highld
56 F7 **Torrin** Highld
46 B3 **Torryburn** Fife
41 K4 **Torthorwald** D & G
36 F4 **Torver** Cumb
7 D6 **Totland** IoW
6 B5 **Totnes** Devon
8 D4 **Totton** Hants
23 G5 **Towcester** Nhants
43 J7 **Tow Law** Dur
47 H6 **Town Yetholm** Border
46 D6 **Traquair** Border
33 H3 **Trawden** Lancs
26 F6 **Trawsfynydd** Gwynd
26 B2 **Trearddur Bay** IoA
20 D7 **Trecastle** Powys
12 C1 **Tredegar** Blae G
2 A8 **Treen** Cnwll
27 G4 **Trefriw** Conwy
19 J1 **Tregaron** Cerdgn
2 F6 **Tregony** Cnwll
19 M6 **Treherbert** Rhondd
12 F2 **Trellech** Mons
26 E5 **Tremadog** Gwynd

43 L7 **Trimdon** Dur
25 J3 **Trimingham** Norfk
14 F3 **Tring** Herts
7 b1 **Trinity** Jersey
45 G5 **Troon** S Ayrs
9 H4 **Trotton** W Susx
37 G3 **Troutbeck** Cumb
13 J5 **Trowbridge** Wilts
2 E6 **Truro** Cnwll
23 H1 **Tugby** Leics
50 D7 **Tullibody** Clacks
50 D2 **Tummel Bridge** P & K
10 E4 **Tunbridge Wells** Kent
17 L2 **Tunstall** Suffk
44 F7 **Turnberry** S Ayrs
29 K5 **Turnditch** Derbys
10 B5 **Turner's Hill** W Susx
60 E4 **Turriff** Abers
23 K5 **Turvey** Bed
29 J6 **Tutbury** Staffs
30 D3 **Tuxford** Notts
22 E1 **Twycross** Leics
8 E4 **Twyford** Hants
14 E6 **Twyford** Wokham
41 G6 **Twynholm** D & G
53 K7 **Tyndrum** Stirlg
43 L5 **Tynemouth** N Tyne
6 F2 **Tytherleigh** Devon
20 A1 **Tywyn** Gwynd

U

10 D6 **Uckfield** E Susx
5 J6 **Uffculme** Devon
14 A5 **Uffington** Oxon
6 A6 **Ugborough** Devon
56 D3 **Uig** Highld
35 H5 **Ulceby** N Linc
42 A7 **Uldale** Cumb
63 G7 **Ullapool** Highld
22 C4 **Ullenhall** Warwks
36 E4 **Ulpha** Cumb
61 c3 **Ulsta** Shet
36 F5 **Ulverston** Cumb
4 F5 **Umberleigh** Devon
63 H4 **Unapool** Highld
13 L5 **Upavon** Wilts
6 F3 **Uplyme** Devon
6 E2 **Uppottery** Devon
9 L5 **Upper Beeding** W Susx
23 K2 **Upper Benefield** Nhants
30 D7 **Upper Broughton** Notts
51 J6 **Upper Largo** Fife
21 K8 **Upper Lydbrook** Gloucs
29 G5 **Upper Tean** Staffs
23 J1 **Uppingham** Rutlnd
11 K3 **Upstreet** Kent
22 A5 **Upton Snodsbury** Worcs
21 M6 **Upton upon Severn** Worcs
13 K5 **Urchfont** Wilts
12 E2 **Usk** Mons
29 H6 **Uttoxeter** Staffs
15 H5 **Uxbridge** Gt Lon
61 d2 **Uyeasound** Shet

V

6 b1 **Vale** Guern
8 F7 **Ventnor** IoW
8 B5 **Verwood** Dorset
61 c4 **Vidlin** Shet
15 G6 **Virginia Water** Surrey
61 c4 **Voe** Shet

W

14 E3 **Waddesdon** Bucks
33 G3 **Waddington** Lancs
30 F4 **Waddington** Lincs
2 F4 **Wadebridge** Cnwll
15 K3 **Wadesmill** Herts
10 E5 **Wadhurst** E Susx
31 K4 **Wainfleet All Saints** Lincs
33 M5 **Wakefield** Wakefd
25 L7 **Walberswick** Suffk
28 E5 **Walgherton** Ches E
46 D6 **Walkerburn** Border

16 B5 **Walkern** Herts
35 G3 **Walkington** E R Yk
32 C7 **Wallasey** Wirral
14 D5 **Wallingford** Oxon
61 b5 **Walls** Shet
22 B1 **Walsall** Wsall
35 J6 **Waltham** NE Lin
16 C7 **Waltham Abbey** Essex
30 E7 **Waltham on the Wolds** Leics
21 G4 **Walton** Powys
12 F7 **Walton** Somset
15 H6 **Walton-on-Thames** Surrey
17 K5 **Walton on the Naze** Essex
45 L6 **Wanlockhead** D & G
23 L1 **Wansford** C Pete
13 H6 **Wanstrow** Somset
14 B5 **Wantage** Oxon
24 A7 **Warboys** Cambs
37 K2 **Warcop** Cumb
29 J3 **Wardlow** Derbys
15 K3 **Ware** Herts
7 L3 **Wareham** Dorset
47 L6 **Warenford** Nthumb
14 E6 **Wargrave** Wokham
42 F4 **Wark** Nthumb
47 H6 **Wark** Nthumb
43 K2 **Warkworth** Nthumb
22 E5 **Warmington** Warwks
13 J6 **Warminster** Wilts
10 B5 **Warninglid** W Susx
32 F7 **Warrington** Warrtn
8 E5 **Warsash** Hants
29 H4 **Warslow** Staffs
32 D4 **Warton** Lancs
22 D4 **Warwick** Warwks
65 b2 **Wasbister** Ork
36 E3 **Wasdale Head** Cumb
30 F3 **Washingborough** Lincs
43 K6 **Washington** Sundld
51 J3 **Watchet** Somset
37 H4 **Watchgate** Cumb
16 D2 **Waterbeach** Cambs
42 A4 **Waterbeck** D & G
29 H5 **Waterhouses** Staffs
9 G5 **Waterlooville** Hants
37 G2 **Watermillock** Cumb
15 H4 **Watford** Herts
23 G4 **Watford** Nhants
34 B6 **Wath upon Dearne** Rothm
14 E4 **Watlington** Oxon
65 H3 **Watten** Highld
24 F5 **Watton** Norfk
15 K2 **Watton-at-Stone** Herts
42 F7 **Wearhead** Dur
24 F4 **Weasenham All Saints** Norfk
28 D3 **Weaverham** Ches W
12 E6 **Wedmore** Somset
23 G4 **Weedon** Nhants
4 B7 **Week St Mary** Cnwll
50 D2 **Weem** P & K
30 F4 **Welbourn** Lincs
22 D5 **Wellesbourne** Warwks
23 J4 **Wellingborough** Nhants
5 K5 **Wellington** Somset
28 D8 **Wellington** Wrekin
12 F6 **Wells** Somset
24 F2 **Wells-next-the-sea** Norfk
24 C6 **Welney** Norfk
28 B6 **Welshampton** Shrops
27 K8 **Welshpool** Powys
23 G4 **Welton** Nhants
15 J3 **Welwyn** Herts
15 J3 **Welwyn Garden City** Herts
28 C6 **Wem** Shrops
15 J5 **Wembley** Gt Lon
3 L6 **Wembury** Devon
14 F3 **Wendover** Bucks
38 B4 **Wensley** N York
34 B5 **Wentbridge** Wakefd
21 H5 **Weobley** Herefs
24 D5 **Wereham** Norfk
38 B2 **West Auckland** Dur
7 H3 **West Bay** Dorset
7 H3 **West Bexington** Dorset
24 E4 **West Bilney** Norfk
30 C6 **West Bridgford** Notts
22 B2 **West Bromwich** Sandw
28 B8 **Westbury** Shrops

13 J6	**Westbury** Wilts	
46 A4	**West Calder** W Loth	
9 K4	**West Chiltington** W Susx	
9 L2	**Westcott** Surrey	
10 C3	**Westerham** Kent	
27 L7	**West Felton** Shrops	
10 F6	**Westfield** E Susx	
23 G3	**West Haddon** Nhants	
10 C5	**West Hoathly** W Susx	
15 H8	**West Horsley** Surrey	
12 D6	**West Huntspill** Somset	
44 F3	**West Kilbride** N Ayrs	
27 K2	**West Kirby** Wirral	
13 K6	**West Lavington** Wilts	
46 C5	**West Linton** Border	
7 L4	**West Lulworth** Dorset	
24 D4	**West Lynn** Norfk	
10 E3	**West Malling** Kent	
21 L5	**West Malvern** Worcs	
9 G4	**West Meon** Hants	
17 H6	**West Mersea** Essex	
8 B5	**West Moors** Dorset	
41 L7	**Westnewton** Cumb	
24 E3	**West Newton** Norfk	
16 B4	**Weston** Herts	
29 G6	**Weston** Staffs	
13 J3	**Westonbirt** Gloucs	
28 E7	**Weston Heath** Shrops	
14 C3	**Weston-on-the-Green** Oxon	
22 C6	**Weston-sub-Edge** Gloucs	
12 D5	**Weston-super-Mare** N Som	
28 D6	**Weston-under-Redcastle** Shrops	
12 F7	**West Pennard** Somset	
2 D5	**West Pentire** Cnwll	
38 D3	**West Rounton** N York	
25 J2	**West Runton** Norfk	
47 G5	**Westruther** Border	
61 c3	**West Sandwick** Shet	
4 D4	**Westward Ho!** Devon	
9 H6	**West Wittering** W Susx	
38 A4	**West Witton** N York	
43 G3	**West Woodburn** Nthumb	
42 C6	**Wetheral** Cumb	
34 B3	**Wetherby** Leeds	
39 J7	**Wetwang** E R Yk	
25 H2	**Weybourne** Norfk	
15 H7	**Weybridge** Surrey	
8 D2	**Weyhill** Hants	
7 J4	**Weymouth** Dorset	
29 G2	**Whaley Bridge** Derbys	
33 G3	**Whalley** Lancs	
31 J7	**Whaplode** Lincs	
31 J7	**Whaplode Drove** Lincs	
40 E6	**Whauphill** D & G	
15 J3	**Wheathampstead** Herts	
14 D3	**Wheatley** Oxon	
5 H4	**Wheddon Cross** Somset	
17 G2	**Whepstead** Suffk	
8 E2	**Wherwell** Hants	
43 J5	**Whickham** Gatesd	
6 A3	**Whiddon Down** Devon	
6 D3	**Whimple** Devon	
15 G3	**Whipsnade** C Beds	
46 A4	**Whitburn** W Loth	
39 H3	**Whitby** N York	
14 E2	**Whitchurch** Bucks	
8 E2	**Whitchurch** Hants	
21 J8	**Whitchurch** Herefs	
28 C5	**Whitchurch** Shrops	
58 D7	**Whitebridge** Highld	
36 D2	**Whitehaven** Cumb	
9 H3	**Whitehill and Bordon** Hants	
60 D3	**Whitehills** Abers	
49 G6	**Whitehouse** Ag & B	
46 F2	**Whitekirk** E Loth	
32 F3	**Whitewell** Lancs	
40 E7	**Whithorn** D & G	
44 E5	**Whiting Bay** N Ayrs	
18 E5	**Whitland** Carmth	
43 K5	**Whitley Bay** N Tyne	
43 G6	**Whitley Chapel** Nthumb	
13 H1	**Whitminster** Gloucs	
11 J2	**Whitstable** Kent	
27 L6	**Whittington** Shrops	
23 G6	**Whittlebury** Nhants	
22 A6	**Whittlesey** Cambs	
21 G4	**Whitton** Powys	
30 B3	**Whitwell** Derbys	
15 J2	**Whitwell** Herts	
65 J3	**Wick** Highld	
16 F7	**Wickford** Essex	
8 F5	**Wickham** Hants	
17 K2	**Wickham Market** Suffk	
13 H3	**Wickwar** S Glos	
43 K3	**Widdrington** Nthumb	
6 A4	**Widecombe in the Moor** Devon	
3 J5	**Widegates** Cnwll	
4 B6	**Widemouth Bay** Cnwll	
16 C5	**Widford** Herts	
30 C6	**Widmerpool** Notts	
28 C2	**Widnes** Halton	
32 E6	**Wigan** Wigan	
24 D4	**Wiggenhall St Germans** Norfk	
23 G1	**Wigston** Leics	
42 A6	**Wigton** Cumb	
40 E6	**Wigtown** D & G	
34 D2	**Wilberfoss** E R Yk	
23 J4	**Wilby** Norfk	
5 J6	**Willand** Devon	
24 B8	**Willingham** Cambs	
22 C4	**Wilmcote** Warwks	
6 F2	**Wilmington** Devon	
28 F2	**Wilmslow** Ches E	
46 A4	**Wilsontown** S Lans	
23 L6	**Wilstead** Bed	
13 L7	**Wilton** Wilts	
24 B6	**Wimblington** Cambs	
8 A5	**Wimborne Minster** Dorset	
13 H7	**Wincanton** Somset	
22 B7	**Winchcombe** Gloucs	
11 G6	**Winchelsea** E Susx	
8 E3	**Winchester** Hants	
37 G4	**Windermere** Cumb	
15 G6	**Windsor** W & M	
14 F2	**Wing** Bucks	
43 L7	**Wingate** Dur	
11 K3	**Wingham** Kent	
14 F6	**Winkfield** Br For	
4 F6	**Winkleigh** Devon	
12 E5	**Winscombe** N Som	
28 D3	**Winsford** Ches W	
5 H4	**Winsford** Somset	
7 G2	**Winsham** Somset	
23 H7	**Winslow** Bucks	
29 J4	**Winster** Derbys	
7 J3	**Winterborne Monkton** Dorset	
7 L2	**Winterborne Stickland** Dorset	
7 L2	**Winterborne Whitechurch** Dorset	
7 J3	**Winterbourne Abbas** Dorset	
13 L7	**Winterbourne Stoke** Wilts	
34 F5	**Winteringham** N Linc	
8 C3	**Winterslow** Wilts	
34 F5	**Winterton** N Linc	
23 L3	**Winwick** Cambs	
29 J4	**Wirksworth** Derbys	
31 K8	**Wisbech** Cambs	
9 K3	**Wisborough Green** W Susx	
45 L3	**Wishaw** N Lans	
16 F5	**Witham** Essex	
5 G6	**Witheridge** Devon	
31 K2	**Withern** Lincs	
35 K4	**Withernsea** E R Yk	
22 B8	**Withington** Gloucs	
21 J6	**Withington** Herefs	
10 D5	**Withyham** E Susx	
5 H4	**Withypool** Somset	
17 J3	**Witnesham** Suffk	
14 B3	**Witney** Oxon	
11 G5	**Wittersham** Kent	
43 J8	**Witton le Wear** Dur	
5 J4	**Wiveliscombe** Somset	
10 C6	**Wivelsfield** E Susx	
17 H5	**Wivenhoe** Essex	
17 J4	**Wix** Essex	
23 K6	**Woburn** C Beds	
15 G7	**Woking** Surrey	
14 F6	**Wokingham** Wokham	
18 C4	**Wolf's Castle** Pembks	
23 J4	**Wollaston** Nhants	
27 L8	**Wollaston** Shrops	
43 H7	**Wolsingham** Dur	
21 M1	**Wolverhampton** Wolves	
22 E2	**Wolvey** Warwks	
38 E2	**Wolviston** S on T	
21 M2	**Wombourne** Staffs	
34 B6	**Wombwell** Barns	
14 F5	**Wooburn** Bucks	
17 K3	**Woodbridge** Suffk	
11 G5	**Woodchurch** Kent	
13 G2	**Woodford** Gloucs	
31 H4	**Woodhall Spa** Lincs	
38 B2	**Woodland** Dur	
14 C3	**Woodstock** Oxon	
21 J4	**Woofferton** Shrops	
12 F6	**Wookey Hole** Somset	
7 L3	**Wool** Dorset	
4 D3	**Woolacombe** Devon	
47 K6	**Wooler** Nthumb	
14 D6	**Woolhampton** W Berk	
17 H2	**Woolpit** Suffk	
28 E5	**Woore** Shrops	
35 G5	**Wootton** N Linc	
14 B2	**Wootton** Oxon	
13 L3	**Wootton Bassett** Wilts	
5 H3	**Wootton Courtenay** Somset	
22 C4	**Wootton Wawen** Warwks	
21 M5	**Worcester** Worcs	
36 D1	**Workington** Cumb	
30 C2	**Worksop** Notts	
17 K1	**Worlingworth** Suffk	
51 J4	**Wormit** Fife	
15 G7	**Worplesdon** Surrey	
21 G1	**Worthen** Shrops	
9 L5	**Worthing** W Susx	
7 M4	**Worth Matravers** Dorset	
13 H3	**Wotton-under-Edge** Gloucs	
31 G3	**Wragby** Lincs	
6 A6	**Wrangaton** Devon	
31 K5	**Wrangle** Lincs	
35 G6	**Wrawby** N Linc	
39 G5	**Wrelton** N York	
25 L7	**Wrentham** Suffk	
16 B3	**Wrestlingworth** C Beds	
27 L5	**Wrexham** Wrexhm	
13 L4	**Wroughton** Swindn	
8 F7	**Wroxall** IoW	
28 D8	**Wroxeter** Shrops	
25 K4	**Wroxham** Norfk	
22 E6	**Wroxton** Oxon	
23 L5	**Wyboston** Bed	
11 H4	**Wye** Kent	
13 K7	**Wylye** Wilts	
30 E7	**Wymondham** Leics	
25 H5	**Wymondham** Norfk	

Y

6 F2	**Yarcombe** Devon	
23 H5	**Yardley Gobion** Nhants	
23 J5	**Yardley Hastings** Nhants	
38 D3	**Yarm** S on T	
8 D6	**Yarmouth** IoW	
46 E6	**Yarrowford** Border	
14 F7	**Yateley** Hants	
12 E5	**Yatton** N Som	
13 J4	**Yatton Keynell** Wilts	
23 M2	**Yaxley** Cambs	
33 K3	**Yeadon** Leeds	
3 L5	**Yealmpton** Devon	
3 L4	**Yelverton** Devon	
25 K5	**Yelverton** Norfk	
7 H1	**Yeovil** Somset	
12 F8	**Yeovilton** Somset	
50 E6	**Yetts o'Muckhart** Clacks	
26 D3	**Y Felinheli** Gwynd	
27 J5	**Y Maerdy** Conwy	
34 C2	**York** C York	
29 J4	**Youlgreave** Derbys	
29 H7	**Yoxall** Staffs	
17 L1	**Yoxford** Suffk	
26 B6	**Y Rhiw** Gwynd	
20 B3	**Ysbyty Ystwyth** Cerdgn	
19 K5	**Ystalyfera** Neath	
19 K5	**Ystradgynlais** Powys	
12 C2	**Ystrad Mynach** Caerph	

Z

13 H7	**Zeals** Wilts	
2 B6	**Zennor** Cnwll	

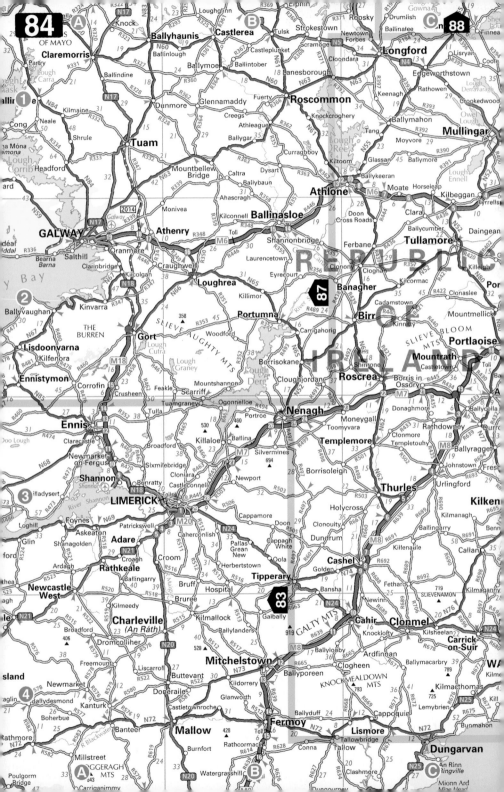

A B C

1

Ceann Iorrais
Erris Head
Cuan an
Inbhir
Mhóir
Downpatrick Head

75
Ballycastle
R314
Killala
Bay
Easky
R297
60
Béal an Mhuirthead
Belmullet
R314
R315
Killala
Inishcrone
51
Carrowmore
Lake
R315
N59
Inis Gé Thuaidh
Inishkea North
Bun na hAbhna
Bunnahowen
R313 19
Bangor
Erris
N59
43
Ballina
Bunnyconnellan
Inis Gé Theas
Inishkea South
719
SLIEVE CARR
Lough
Conn
N59
Slieve Gamph or
31
Dubh Oileán Mór
*Duvillaun
More*
Cuan an
Fhóid Dhuibh
Blacksod Bay
31
806
NEPHIN
R312
R310
N26
Tob
671
SLIEVEMORE
R319
55
R315
Foxford
Charles
Achill
Head
Keel
NEPHIN BEG RANGE
N59
R317
13
Swinford
Achill Island
Oileán Acla
27
Mulrany
Lough
Feeagh
R317
R312
R310
24
Kilkel
Kiltamagh
29
R311
Turlough
29
N5
Clew Bay
Newport
Castlebar
R324
Balla
N60
R320
R3
Clare Island
31
Westport
17
N5
Ballyhean
29
PLAINS
OF MAYO
14
Kn
Louisburgh
R335
21
762
CROAGH PATRICK
R330
29
N84
Claremorris
R331
19
R378
32
Partry
Lough
Carra
21
Ballind
Inishturk
Caher
Island
31
R335
32
Lough
Mask
673
R330
Ballinrobe
N84
Kilmaine
31
N17
2
Inishbofin
Renvyle
N59
Leenane
Cong
Neale
R332
Inishshark
Letterfrack
R344
14
An Fhairche
Clonbur
50
Shrule
R334
R379
34
R336
Corr na Móna
Cornamona
R345
64
R333
Clifden
N59
19
Sraith Salach
Recess
16
R336
Lough
Corrib
Headford
32
Ballyconneely
R342
Cashel
R340
Oughterard
N84
Slyne Head
R341
42
Roundstone
Glinsce
Glinsk
43
N59
Galway
N17
Cruach na Caoile
*Croaghnakeela
Island*
Cárna
Cárna
47
Cill Chiaráin
Kilkieran
GALWAY
Garumna
*Gorumna
Island*
An Spidéal
Spiddal
R336
Bearna
Barna
Salthill
Oran
Clarinbridge
An Sunda ó Thuaidh
North Sound
Galway Bay
Inis Mór
Inishmore
Kinvarra
R347
Inis Meáin
Inishmaan
Ballyvaughan
30
R471
R67
THE
BURREN
Oileáin Árann
Aran Islands
Inis Óirr
Inisheer
South
Sound
Doolin
Lisdoonvarna
M18
R478
R481
Kilfenora
R476
R460
16
Ennistymon
Liscannor
R478
Corrofin
15
Hags Head
Lahinch
N85
45
Cr

Milltown Malbay
Mal Bay
R474
R460
31
Ennis
Spanish Point
Clarecastle
R47
Doo Lough
R68
Newmarket-
on-Fergus

A B C

3

4

Doonbeg

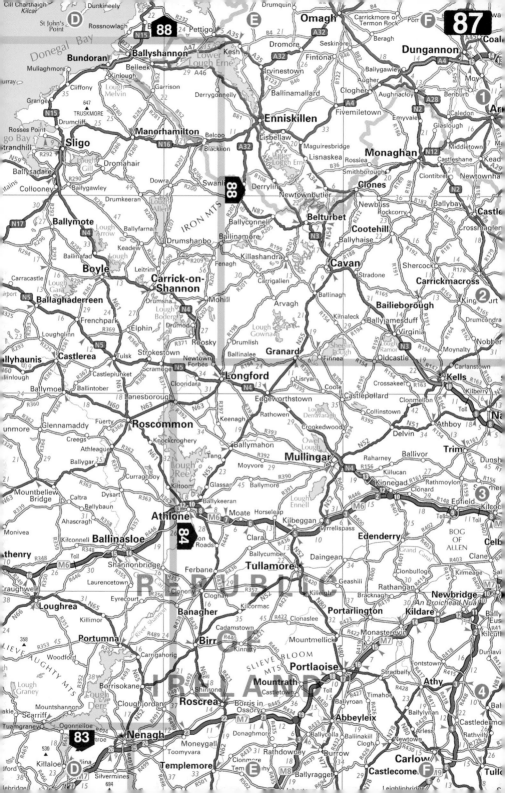

Mileage chart - Ireland

The mileage chart shows distances in miles between two towns along AA-recommended routes. Using motorways and other main roads this is normally the fastest route, though not necessarily the shortest.

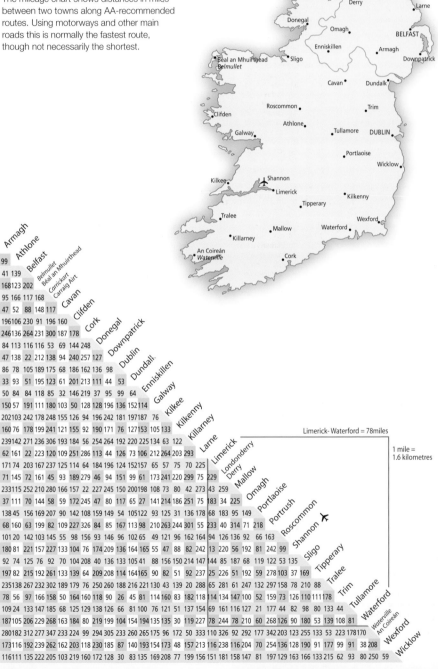

Limerick- Waterford = 78miles

1 mile = 1.6 kilometres

Armagh	Athlone	Belfast	Belmullet / Béal an Mhuirhead	Carrickart / Carraig Airt	Cavan	Clifden	Cork	Donegal	Downpatrick	Dublin	Dundalk	Enniskillen	Galway	Kilkee	Kilkenny	Killarney	Larne	Limerick	Londonderry / Derry	Mallow	Omagh	Portlaoise	Portrush	Roscommon	Shannon	Sligo	Tipperary	Tralee	Trim	Tullamore	Waterford	Waterville / An Coireán	Wexford	Wicklow
99																																		
41	139																																	
168	123	202																																
95	166	117	168																															
47	52	88	148	117																														
196	106	230	91	196	160																													
246	136	264	231	300	187	178																												
84	113	116	116	53	69	144	248																											
47	138	22	212	138	94	240	257	127																										
86	78	105	189	175	68	186	162	136	98																									
33	93	51	195	123	61	201	213	111	44	53																								
50	84	84	118	85	32	146	219	37	95	99	64																							
150	57	191	111	180	103	50	128	128	196	136	152	114																						
202	103	242	178	248	155	126	94	196	242	181	197	187	76																					
160	76	178	199	241	121	155	92	190	171	76	127	153	105	133																				
239	142	271	236	306	193	184	56	254	264	192	220	225	134	63	122																			
62	161	22	223	120	109	251	286	113	44	126	73	106	212	264	203	293																		
171	74	145	237	125	114	64	184	196	124	152	157	65	57	75	70	225																		
71	145	72	161	45	93	189	279	46	94	151	99	61	173	241	220	299	75	229																
233	115	252	210	280	166	157	22	227	245	150	200	198	108	73	80	42	273	43	259															
37	111	70	144	58	59	172	245	47	80	117	65	27	141	214	186	251	75	183	34	225														
138	45	156	169	207	90	142	108	159	149	54	105	122	93	125	31	136	178	68	183	95	149													
68	160	63	199	82	109	227	326	84	85	167	113	98	210	263	244	301	55	233	40	314	71	218												
101	20	142	103	145	55	98	156	93	146	96	102	65	49	121	96	162	164	94	126	136	92	66	163											
180	81	221	157	227	133	104	76	174	209	136	164	165	55	47	88	82	242	13	220	56	192	81	242	99										
92	74	125	76	92	70	104	208	40	136	133	105	41	88	156	150	214	147	144	85	187	68	119	122	53	135									
197	82	215	192	261	133	139	64	209	208	114	164	165	90	82	51	92	237	25	226	51	192	59	278	103	37	169								
235	138	267	232	302	189	179	76	250	260	188	216	221	130	43	139	20	288	65	281	61	247	132	297	158	78	210	88							
78	56	97	166	158	50	164	169	118	90	26	45	81	114	160	83	182	118	114	134	147	100	52	159	73	126	110	111	178						
109	24	133	147	185	68	125	129	138	126	66	81	100	76	121	51	137	154	69	161	116	127	21	177	44	82	98	80	133	44					
187	105	206	229	268	163	184	80	219	199	104	154	194	135	135	30	119	227	78	244	78	210	60	268	126	90	180	53	139	108	81				
280	182	312	277	347	233	224	99	294	305	230	260	265	175	96	172	50	333	110	326	92	292	177	342	203	123	255	133	53	223	178	170			
173	116	192	239	262	162	203	118	230	185	87	140	193	154	173	48	157	213	116	238	116	204	70	254	136	128	190	91	177	99	91	38	208		
116	111	135	222	205	103	219	160	172	128	30	83	135	169	208	77	199	156	151	181	158	147	81	197	129	163	166	133	215	62	93	80	250	59	

A

82 C2 **Abbeydorney** Kerry
82 C3 **Abbeyfeale** Limrck
84 C3 **Abbeyleix** Laois
85 D4 **Adamstown** Wexfd
83 D2 **Adare** Limrck
82 C3 **Adrigole** Cork
89 D2 **Aghadowey** Lderry
87 D3 **Ahascragh** Galway
89 D2 **Ahoghill** Antrim
82 B3 **Allihies** Cork
88 B2 **Anascaul** Kerry
88 B2 **An Bun Beag** Donegl
88 A2 **An Charraig** Donegl
88 A2 **An Clochán Liath**
　　　 Donegl
82 B3 **An Coireán** Kerry
82 B2 **An Daingean** Kerry
86 C3 **An Fhairche** Galway
89 E4 **Annalong** Down
84 C4 **Annestown** Watfd
83 F3 **An Rinn** Watfd
86 C3 **An Spidéal** Galway
89 D2 **Antrim** Antrim
83 D2 **Ardagh** Limrck
88 A2 **Ardara** Donegl
89 D4 **Ardee** Louth
82 C2 **Ardfert** Kerry
84 C4 **Ardfinnan** Tippry
89 E3 **Ardglass** Down
82 B3 **Ardgroom** Cork
83 E3 **Ardmore** Watfd
85 E3 **Arklow** Wicklw
85 D3 **Arless** Laois
89 D3 **Armagh** Armagh
89 D1 **Armoy** Antrim
85 D4 **Arthurstown** Wexfd
88 B4 **Arvagh** Cavan
85 E1 **Ashbourne** Meath
85 E2 **Ashford** Wicklw
83 D1 **Askeaton** Limrck
85 D1 **Athboy** Meath
82 C2 **Athea** Limrck
87 D3 **Athenry** Galway
87 D3 **Athleague** Roscom
84 C1 **Athlone** Wmeath
85 D2 **Athy** Kildre
88 C3 **Augher** Tyrone
88 C3 **Aughnacloy** Tyrone
85 E3 **Aughrim** Wicklw
85 E3 **Avoca** Wicklw

B

85 D3 **Bagenalstown** Carlow
82 C3 **Baile Mhic Íre** Cork
88 C4 **Bailieborough** Cavan
85 E1 **Balbriggan** Dublin
86 C2 **Balla** Mayo
87 D2 **Ballaghaderreen**
　　　 Roscom
86 C2 **Ballina** Mayo
83 D1 **Ballina** Tippry
87 D2 **Ballinafad** Sligo
88 C4 **Ballinagh** Cavan
84 C3 **Ballinakill** Laois
88 B4 **Ballinalee** Longfd
88 B3 **Ballinamallard**
　　　 Ferman
88 B4 **Ballinamore** Leitrm
83 D3 **Ballinascarty** Cork

84 B2 **Ballinasloe** Galway
86 C3 **Ballindine** Mayo
83 D3 **Ballineen** Cork
83 D2 **Ballingarry** Limrck
84 C3 **Ballingarry** Tippry
82 C3 **Ballinspittle** Cork
83 D3 **Ballinhassig** Cork
87 D2 **Ballinlough** Roscom
86 C3 **Ballinrobe** Mayo
83 D3 **Ballinspittle** Cork
87 D2 **Ballintober** Roscom
88 B3 **Ballintra** Donegl
85 D1 **Ballivor** Meath
85 D3 **Ballon** Carlow
87 D3 **Ballybaun** Galway
88 C4 **Ballybay** Monhan
88 B2 **Ballybofey** Donegl
82 C2 **Ballybunion** Kerry
85 E3 **Ballycanew** Wexfd
89 E2 **Ballycarry** Antrim
89 D1 **Ballycastle** Antrim
86 C1 **Ballycastle** Mayo
89 E2 **Ballyclare** Antrim
84 C3 **Ballycolla** Laois
86 B3 **Ballyconneely** Galway
88 B4 **Ballyconnell** Cavan
83 E3 **Ballycotton** Cork
84 C2 **Ballycumber** Offaly
82 C4 **Ballydehob** Cork
82 C2 **Ballydesmond** Cork
82 C2 **Ballyduff** Kerry
84 B4 **Ballyduff** Watfd
87 D2 **Ballyfarnan** Roscom
89 E2 **Ballygalley** Antrim
87 D3 **Ballygar** Galway
87 D1 **Ballygawley** Sligo
88 C3 **Ballygawley** Tyrone
89 E3 **Ballygowan** Down
85 D4 **Ballyhack** Wexfd
88 C4 **Ballyhaise** Cavan
85 D3 **Ballyhale** Kilken
87 D2 **Ballyhaunis** Mayo
86 C2 **Ballyhean** Mayo
82 B2 **Ballyheige** Kerry
88 C4 **Ballyjamesduff** Cavan
84 C1 **Ballykeeran** Wmeath
83 E2 **Ballylanders** Limrck
82 C3 **Ballylickey** Cork
88 C1 **Ballyliffin** Donegl
82 C2 **Ballylongford** Kerry
84 B4 **Ballylooby** Tippry
85 D2 **Ballylynan** Laois
84 C4 **Ballymacarbry** Watfd
84 C1 **Ballymahon** Longfd
82 C3 **Ballymakeery** Cork
89 D2 **Ballymena** Antrim
87 D2 **Ballymoe** Galway
89 D2 **Ballymoney** Antrim
84 C1 **Ballymore** Wmeath
85 D2 **Ballymore Eustace**
　　　 Kildre
87 D2 **Ballymote** Sligo
89 E3 **Ballynahinch** Down
89 E2 **Ballynure** Antrim
84 B4 **Ballyporeen** Tippry
84 C3 **Ballyragget** Kilken
84 C2 **Ballyroan** Laois
89 D2 **Ballyronan** Lderry
87 D1 **Ballysadare** Sligo
87 D1 **Ballyshannon** Donegl
86 C4 **Ballyvaughan** Clare
89 E3 **Ballywalter** Down
85 E1 **Balrothery** Dublin
82 C4 **Baltimore** Cork
85 D2 **Baltinglass** Wicklw

84 B2 **Banagher** Offaly
89 D3 **Banbridge** Down
83 D3 **Bandon** Cork
89 E2 **Bangor** Down
86 B2 **Bangor Erris** Mayo
84 B3 **Bansha** Tippry
83 D2 **Banteer** Cork
82 C3 **Bantry** Cork
86 C3 **Barna** Galway
86 B1 **Béal an Mhuirthead**
　　　 Mayo
82 C3 **Béal Átha an**
　　　 Ghaorthaidh Cork
86 C3 **Bearna** Galway
82 C3 **Beaufort** Kerry
87 E1 **Belcoo** Ferman
89 E3 **Belfast** Belfst
83 D3 **Belgooly** Cork
89 D2 **Bellaghy** Lderry
87 D1 **Belleek** Ferman
86 B1 **Belmullet** Mayo
88 C4 **Belturbet** Cavan
89 D3 **Benburb** Tyrone
85 D3 **Bennettsbridge**
　　　 Kilken
88 C3 **Beragh** Tyrone
85 E1 **Bettystown** Meath
84 C2 **Birr** Offaly
87 E1 **Blacklion** Cavan
85 E2 **Blackrock** Dublin
85 E3 **Blackwater** Wexfd
83 D3 **Blarney** Cork
85 D2 **Blessington** Wicklw
83 D2 **Boherbue** Cork
85 D3 **Borris** Carlow
84 C2 **Borris in Ossory** Laois
87 D4 **Borrisokane** Tippry
84 C3 **Borrisoleigh** Tippry
87 D2 **Boyle** Roscom
84 B2 **Bracknagh** Offaly
85 E2 **Bray** Wicklw
85 D4 **Bridgetown** Wexfd
85 E2 **Brittas** Dublin
83 D1 **Broadford** Clare
83 D2 **Broadford** Limrck
89 D2 **Broughshane** Antrim
83 D2 **Bruff** Limrck
83 D2 **Bruree** Limrck
88 B2 **Bunbeg** Donegl
85 D3 **Bunclody** Wexfd
88 C1 **Buncrana** Donegl
87 D1 **Bundoran** Donegl
84 C4 **Bunmahon** Watfd
86 B1 **Bun na hAbhna** Mayo
86 B1 **Bunnahowen** Mayo
86 C2 **Bunnyconnellan**
　　　 Mayo
83 D1 **Bunratty** Clare
83 D3 **Burnfort** Cork
89 D1 **Bushmills** Antrim
83 D2 **Buttevant** Cork

C

84 C2 **Cadamstown** Offaly
83 D1 **Caherconlish** Limrck
82 B3 **Caherdaniel** Kerry
82 B3 **Cahersiveen** Kerry
84 C4 **Cahir** Tippry
88 C3 **Caledon** Tyrone
84 C3 **Callan** Kilken
87 D3 **Caltra** Galway
82 B2 **Camp** Kerry

85 D4 **Campile** Wexfd
84 B3 **Cappagh White**
　　　 Tippry
83 E1 **Cappamore** Limrck
84 C4 **Cappoquin** Watfd
85 D1 **Carlanstown** Meath
89 D4 **Carlingford** Louth
85 D3 **Carlow** Carlow
86 B3 **Carna** Galway
88 C1 **Carndonagh** Donegl
85 E3 **Carnew** Wicklw
89 E2 **Carnlough** Antrim
87 D2 **Carracastle** Mayo
88 B1 **Carraig Airt** Donegl
88 A2 **Carrick** Donegl
88 B1 **Carrickart** Donegl
89 E2 **Carrickfergus** Antrim
89 D4 **Carrickmacross**
　　　 Monhan
88 C3 **Carrickmore or**
　　　 Termon Rock Tyrone
87 D2 **Carrick-on-Shannon**
　　　 Leitrm
84 C4 **Carrick-on-Suir** Tippry
87 D4 **Carrigahorig** Tippry
83 D3 **Carrigaline** Cork
88 B4 **Carrigallen** Leitrm
88 D3 **Carriganimmy** Cork
88 C2 **Carrigans** Donegl
83 E3 **Carrigtohill** Cork
89 E3 **Carryduff** Down
86 B3 **Cashel** Galway
84 C3 **Cashel** Tippry
86 C2 **Castlebar** Mayo
89 D4 **Castlebellingham**
　　　 Louth
89 D4 **Castleblayney**
　　　 Monhan
85 E4 **Castlebridge** Wexfd
85 D3 **Castlecomer** Kilken
83 D1 **Castleconnell** Limrck
88 B2 **Castlederg** Tyrone
85 D2 **Castledermot** Kildre
82 B2 **Castlegregory** Kerry
82 C2 **Castleisland** Kerry
82 C2 **Castlemaine** Kerry
83 E3 **Castlemartyr** Cork
87 D2 **Castleplunket**
　　　 Roscom
84 C1 **Castlepollard**
　　　 Wmeath
87 D2 **Castlerea** Roscom
88 C1 **Castlerock** Lderry
88 C3 **Castleshane** Monhan
84 C2 **Castletown** Laois
82 B3 **Castletown**
　　　 Bearhaven Cork
83 D2 **Castletownroche**
　　　 Cork
82 C2 **Castletownshend**
　　　 Cork
89 E3 **Castlewellan** Down
82 B3 **Cathair Dónall** Kerry
82 C2 **Causeway** Kerry
88 C4 **Cavan** Cavan
85 D2 **Celbridge** Kildre
86 C2 **Charlestown** Mayo
83 D2 **Charleville** Cork
85 D4 **Cheekpoint** Watfd
88 A2 **Cill Charthaigh**
　　　 Donegl
86 B3 **Cill Chiaráin** Galway
88 C2 **Clady** Tyrone
85 D2 **Clane** Kildre
84 C2 **Clara** Offaly

83 D1 Clarecastle Clare
86 C2 Claremorris Mayo
86 C3 Clarinbridge Galway
83 E3 Clashmore Watfd
88 C2 Claudy Lderry
86 B3 Clifden Galway
87 D1 Cliffony Sligo
85 D3 Clogh Kilken
84 C2 Cloghan Offaly
84 B4 Clogheen Tippry
88 C3 Clogher Tyrone
85 D3 Clohamon Wexfd
83 D4 Clonakilty Cork
85 D1 Clonard Meath
84 C2 Clonaslee Laois
85 D2 Clonbulloge Offaly
86 C3 Clonbur Galway
85 E2 Clondalkin Dublin
88 C3 Clones Monhan
83 D1 Clonlara Clare
88 C1 Clonmany Donegl
84 C4 Clonmel Tippry
85 D1 Clonmellon Wmeath
84 C3 Clonmore Tippry
84 C2 Clonony Offaly
84 C3 Clonoulty Tippry
85 D3 Clonroche Wexfd
88 C3 Clontibret Monhan
84 C1 Cloondara Longfd
89 E3 Clough Down
87 E4 Cloughjordan Tippry
83 E3 Cloyne Cork
89 D2 Coagh Tyrone
89 D3 Coalisland Tyrone
83 E3 Cobh Cork
89 D1 Coleraine Lderry
85 D1 Collinstown Wmeath
89 D4 Collon Louth
87 D1 Collooney Sligo
89 E3 Comber Down
86 C3 Cong Mayo
83 E3 Conna Cork
89 D2 Cookstown Tyrone
84 C1 Coole Wmeath
82 C1 Cooraclare Clare
88 C4 Cootehill Cavan
83 D3 Cork Cork
86 C3 Cornamona Galway
86 C3 Corr na Móna Galway
86 C4 Corrofin Clare
83 D3 Courtmacsherry Cork
85 E3 Courtown Wexfd
89 D3 Craigavon Armagh
87 D3 Craughwell Galway
89 E2 Crawfordsburn Down
87 D3 Creegs Galway
88 B1 Creeslough Donegl
83 D2 Croagh Limrck
88 B2 Croithli Donegl
88 B2 Crolly Donegl
84 C1 Crookedwood Wmeath
82 C4 Crookhaven Cork
83 D3 Crookstown Cork
83 D2 Croom Limrck
85 D1 Crossakeel Meath
83 D3 Cross Barry Cork
83 E3 Crosshaven Cork
89 D4 Crossmaglen Armagh
86 C2 Crossmolina Mayo
89 D2 Crumlin Antrim
86 C4 Crusheen Clare
88 C1 Culdaff Donegl
89 D2 Cullybackey Antrim
85 E4 Curracloe Wexfd

87 D3 Curraghboy Roscom
87 D2 Curry Sligo
89 D2 Cushendall Antrim
89 D1 Cushendun Antrim

D

84 C2 Daingean Offaly
85 E2 Delgany Wicklw
85 D1 Delvin Wmeath
88 C2 Derry Lderry
87 E1 Derrygonnelly Ferman
88 B3 Derrylin Ferman
87 D2 Dervock Antrim
82 B2 Dingle Kerry
89 D2 Doagh Antrim
89 E2 Donaghadee Down
84 C3 Donaghmore Laois
85 D2 Donard Wicklw
88 B2 Donegal Donegl
83 D2 Doneraile Cork
86 C4 Doolin Clare
83 E1 Doon Limrck
82 C1 Doonbeg Clare
84 C2 Doon Cross Roads Offaly
83 D3 Douglas Cork
89 E3 Downpatrick Down
87 E1 Dowra Cavan
89 D2 Draperstown Lderry
82 C3 Drimoleague Cork
83 D3 Dripsey Cork
85 E1 Drogheda Louth
87 D1 Dromahair Leitrm
83 D2 Dromcolliher Limrck
89 D3 Dromore Down
88 C3 Dromore Tyrone
86 C1 Dromore West Sligo
87 D1 Drumcliff Sligo
89 D4 Drumconda Meath
87 D1 Drumkeeran Leitrm
88 B4 Drumlish Longfd
87 E2 Drumod Leitrm
88 C3 Drumquin Tyrone
87 E2 Drumshanbo Leitrm
87 E2 Drumsna Leitrm
82 C2 Duagh Kerry
85 E2 Dublin Dublin
85 E1 Duleek Meath
85 E1 Dunboyne Meath
85 D4 Duncormick Wexfd
89 D4 Dundalk Louth
89 D3 Dunderrow Cork
89 E3 Dundonald Down
89 E3 Dundrum Down
84 B3 Dundrum Tippry
88 B1 Dunfanaghy Donegl
89 D3 Dungannon Tyrone
85 D3 Dungarvan Kilken
83 F3 Dungarvan Watfd
88 C2 Dungiven Lderry
88 A2 Dunglow Donegl
83 E3 Dungourney Cork
88 A2 Dunkineely Donegl
85 E2 Dún Laoghaire Dublin
85 D2 Dunlavin Wicklw
89 D4 Dunleer Louth
89 D2 Dunloy Antrim
82 C3 Dunmanway Cork
87 D3 Dunmore Galway
85 D4 Dunmore East Watfd
89 E3 Dunmurry Antrim

85 D1 Dunshaughlin Meath
84 C3 Durrow Laois
82 C4 Durrus Cork
87 D3 Dysart Roscom

E

86 C1 Easky Sligo
85 D2 Edenderry Offaly
84 C1 Edgeworthstown Longfd
88 C2 Eglinton Lderry
87 D2 Elphin Roscom
88 C3 Emyvale Monhan
85 D1 Enfield Meath
83 D1 Ennis Clare
85 D3 Enniscorthy Wexfd
83 D3 Enniskean Cork
88 B3 Enniskillen Ferman
86 C4 Ennistymon Clare
87 D4 Eyrecourt Galway

F

88 C2 Fahan Donegl
82 C2 Farranfore Kerry
87 D4 Feakle Clare
87 E2 Fenagh Leitrm
84 C2 Ferbane Offaly
83 E2 Fermoy Cork
85 E3 Ferns Wexfd
84 C3 Fethard Tippry
85 D4 Fethard Wexfd
88 C4 Finnea Wmeath
88 C3 Fintona Tyrone
88 C3 Fivemiletown Tyrone
85 D2 Fontstown Kildre
85 D4 Foulkesmill Wexfd
86 C2 Foxford Mayo
83 D1 Foynes Limrck
83 D2 Freemount Cork
87 D2 Frenchpark Roscom
84 C3 Freshford Kilken
87 D3 Fuerty Roscom

G

83 E2 Galbally Limrck
86 C3 Galway Galway
87 D1 Garrison Ferman
85 E1 Garristown Dublin
83 E3 Garryvoe Cork
89 D2 Garvagh Lderry
84 C2 Geashill Offaly
89 D3 Gilford Down
82 C4 Glandore Cork
83 D3 Glanmire Cork
83 E2 Glanworth Cork
88 C3 Glaslough Monhan
84 C1 Glassan Wmeath
88 A2 Gleann Cholm Cille Donegl
89 E2 Glenarm Antrim
89 D3 Glenavy Antrim
82 B3 Glenbeigh Kerry
88 A2 Glencolumbkille Donegl
85 E2 Glenealy Wicklw
82 C3 Glengarriff Cork

85 D4 Glenmore Kilken
87 D3 Glennamaddy Galway
88 B2 Glenties Donegl
82 C2 Glin Limrck
86 B3 Glinsce Galway
86 B3 Glinsk Galway
84 B3 Golden Tippry
82 C4 Goleen Cork
85 D3 Goresbridge Kilken
85 E3 Gorey Wexfd
86 C4 Gort Galway
88 C2 Gortin Tyrone
85 D3 Gowran Kilken
85 D3 Graiguenamanagh Kilken
88 C4 Granard Longfd
87 D1 Grange Sligo
89 D4 Greenore Louth
89 E3 Greyabbey Down
85 E2 Greystones Wicklw
89 D2 Gulladuff Lderry

H

85 D3 Hacketstown Carlow
86 C3 Headford Galway
83 D2 Herbertstown Limrck
89 D3 Hillsborough Down
89 D3 Hilltown Down
84 C3 Holycross Tippry
89 E2 Holywood Down
84 C1 Horseleap Wmeath
83 D2 Hospital Limrck
85 E1 Howth Dublin

I

82 B2 Inch Kerry
82 C3 Inchigeelagh Cork
83 D3 Inishannon Cork
86 C1 Inishcrone Sligo
85 D3 Inistioge Kilken
88 B3 Irvinestown Ferman

J

84 C3 Johnstown Kilken

K

83 D2 Kanturk Cork
87 D2 Keadew Roscom
89 D3 Keady Armagh
86 B2 Keel Mayo
84 C1 Keenagh Longfd
89 D2 Kells Antrim
85 D1 Kells Meath
82 C3 Kenmare Kerry
88 B3 Kesh Ferman
84 C2 Kilbeggan Wmeath
85 D1 Kilberry Meath
83 D3 Kilbrittain Cork
88 A2 Kilcar Donegl
85 D1 Kilcock Kildre
86 C4 Kilcolgan Galway
87 D3 Kilconnell Galway
85 E2 Kilcoole Wicklw

84 C2 **Kilcormac** Offaly
85 D2 **Kilcullen** Kildre
89 D4 **Kilcurry** Louth
85 D2 **Kildare** Kildre
85 D3 **Kildavin** Carlow
83 D2 **Kildorrery** Cork
86 C4 **Kilfenora** Clare
82 C3 **Kilgarvan** Kerry
82 C1 **Kilkee** Clare
89 E4 **Kilkeel** Down
86 C2 **Kilkelly** Mayo
84 C3 **Kilkenny** Kilken
86 B3 **Kilkieran** Galway
82 C2 **Kilkinlea Lower** Limrck
85 D2 **Kill** Kildre
84 C4 **Kill** Watfd
83 D1 **Killadysert** Clare
86 C1 **Killala** Mayo
83 D1 **Killaloe** Clare
82 C3 **Killarney** Kerry
88 C4 **Killashandra** Cavan
83 E3 **Killeagh** Cork
84 C2 **Killeigh** Offaly
84 C3 **Killenaule** Tippry
82 C1 **Killimer** Clare
87 D4 **Killimor** Galway
85 E2 **Killiney** Dublin
85 E4 **Killinick** Wexfd
82 C2 **Killorglin** Kerry
89 E3 **Killough** Down
85 D1 **Killucan** Wmeath
88 A2 **Killybegs** Donegl
89 E3 **Killyleagh** Down
85 E2 **Kilmacanoge** Wicklw
88 B2 **Kilmacrenan** Donegl
84 C4 **Kilmacthomas** Watfd
84 C3 **Kilmaganny** Kilken
86 C3 **Kilmaine** Mayo
83 D2 **Kilmallock** Limrck
84 C3 **Kilmanagh** Kilken
84 C4 **Kilmeadan** Watfd
85 D2 **Kilmeage** Kildre
83 D2 **Kilmeedy** Limrck
83 D3 **Kilmichael** Cork
85 D4 **Kilmore Quay** Wexfd
85 E3 **Kilmuckridge** Wexfd
88 C4 **Kilnaleck** Cavan
89 D2 **Kilrea** Lderry
82 C1 **Kilrush** Clare
84 C4 **Kilsheelan** Tippry
86 C2 **Kiltamagh** Mayo
85 D3 **Kiltealy** Wexfd
85 D3 **Kiltegan** Wicklw
87 E3 **Kiltoom** Roscom
89 D4 **Kingscourt** Cavan
87 D1 **Kinlough** Leitrm
85 D1 **Kinnegad** Wmeath
84 C2 **Kinnitty** Offaly
83 D3 **Kinsale** Cork
86 C4 **Kinvarra** Galway
89 E3 **Kircubbin** Down
86 C2 **Knock** Mayo
87 D3 **Knockcroghery** Roscom
84 C4 **Knocklofty** Tippry
85 D3 **Knocktopher** Kilken

L

86 C4 **Lahinch** Clare

84 B1 **Lanesborough** Roscom
85 E2 **Laragh** Wicklw
89 E2 **Larne** Antrim
82 C3 **Lauragh** Kerry
87 D3 **Laurencetown** Galway
82 C4 **Leap** Cork
86 B3 **Leenane** Galway
85 D3 **Leighlinbridge** Carlow
87 D2 **Leitrim** Leitrm
85 D2 **Leixlip** Kildre
84 C4 **Lemybrien** Watfd
86 B3 **Letterfrack** Galway
88 B2 **Letterkenny** Donegl
88 C2 **Lifford** Donegl
88 C2 **Limavady** Lderry
83 D1 **Limerick** Limrck
88 C3 **Lisbellaw** Ferman
89 D3 **Lisburn** Antrim
86 C4 **Liscannor** Clare
83 D2 **Liscarroll** Cork
86 C4 **Lisdoonvarna** Clare
84 C4 **Lismore** Watfd
88 C3 **Lisnaskea** Ferman
84 C1 **Lisryan** Longfd
82 C2 **Listowel** Kerry
82 C1 **Loghill** Limrck
88 C2 **Londonderry** Lderry
84 C1 **Longford** Longfd
89 D3 **Loughbrickland** Down
89 D3 **Loughgall** Armagh
87 D2 **Loughglinn** Roscom
87 D4 **Loughrea** Galway
86 B2 **Louisburgh** Mayo
85 E2 **Lucan** Dublin
89 D3 **Lurgan** Armagh
85 E1 **Lusk** Dublin

M

88 B1 **Machair Loiscthe** Donegl
83 D3 **Macroom** Cork
89 E3 **Maghera** Down
89 D2 **Maghera** Lderry
89 D2 **Magherafelt** Lderry
88 C3 **Maguiresbridge** Ferman
85 E1 **Malahide** Dublin
88 A2 **Málainn Mhóir** Donegl
88 C1 **Malin** Donegl
88 A2 **Malin More** Donegl
83 D2 **Mallow** Cork
87 D1 **Manorhamilton** Leitrm
89 D3 **Markethill** Armagh
89 D2 **Martinstown** Antrim
85 D1 **Maynooth** Kildre
89 D3 **Mazetown** Antrim
88 C3 **Middletown** Armagh
83 E3 **Midleton** Cork
88 B2 **Millford** Donegl
83 D3 **Millstreet** Cork
82 C2 **Milltown** Kerry
82 C1 **Milltown Malbay** Clare
83 E2 **Mitchelstown** Cork
84 C1 **Moate** Wmeath
87 E2 **Mohill** Leitrm
88 C3 **Monaghan** Monhan
85 D2 **Monasterevin** Kildre
84 C3 **Moneygall** Offaly

89 D2 **Moneymore** Lderry
87 D3 **Monivea** Galway
84 C4 **Mooncoin** Kilken
89 D2 **Moorfields** Antrim
87 D3 **Mountbellew Bridge** Galway
88 B2 **Mountcharles** Donegl
84 C2 **Mountmellick** Laois
84 C2 **Mountrath** Laois
87 D4 **Mountshannon** Clare
88 C1 **Moville** Donegl
89 D3 **Moy** Tyrone
88 C4 **Moynalty** Meath
84 C1 **Moyvore** Wmeath
82 C3 **Muckross** Kerry
88 C2 **Muff** Donegl
87 D1 **Mullaghmore** Sligo
85 D4 **Mullinavat** Kilken
84 C1 **Mullingar** Wmeath
86 B2 **Mulrany** Mayo
85 D3 **Myshall** Carlow

N

85 D2 **Naas** Kildre
85 E1 **Naul** Dublin
85 D1 **Navan** Meath
86 C3 **Neale** Mayo
83 E1 **Nenagh** Tippry
88 C3 **Newbliss** Monhan
85 D2 **Newbridge** Kildre
89 E3 **Newcastle** Down
83 D2 **Newcastle West** Limrck
84 C4 **Newinn** Tippry
83 D2 **Newmarket** Cork
83 D1 **Newmarket-on-Fergus** Clare
86 B2 **Newport** Mayo
83 D1 **Newport** Tippry
85 D4 **New Ross** Wexfd
89 D3 **Newry** Down
85 D3 **Newtown** Laois
89 E2 **Newtownabbey** Antrim
89 E3 **Newtownards** Down
88 C3 **Newtownbutler** Ferman
84 C1 **Newtown Forbes** Longfd
89 D3 **Newtownhamilton** Armagh
85 E2 **Newtown Mount Kennedy** Wicklw
88 C2 **Newtownstewart** Tyrone
89 D4 **Nobber** Meath

O

83 D1 **Ogonnelloe** Clare
85 D4 **Oilgate** Wexfd
88 C4 **Oldcastle** Meath
88 C3 **Omagh** Tyrone
89 D4 **Omeath** Louth
83 E2 **Oola** Limrck
86 C3 **Oranmore** Galway
86 C3 **Oughterard** Galway

83 D3 **Ovens** Cork

P

83 E2 **Pallas Green New** Limrck
82 B3 **Parknasilla** Kerry
86 C2 **Partry** Mayo
85 D4 **Passage East** Watfd
83 E3 **Passage West** Cork
83 D1 **Patrickswell** Limrck
85 D3 **Paulstown** Kilken
88 B3 **Pettigo** Donegl
88 C2 **Plumbridge** Tyrone
88 C3 **Pomeroy** Tyrone
89 D3 **Portadown** Armagh
89 E3 **Portaferry** Down
85 D2 **Portarlington** Laois
89 E3 **Portavogie** Down
89 D1 **Portballintrae** Antrim
89 D2 **Portglenone** Antrim
84 C2 **Portlaoise** Laois
85 E1 **Portmarnock** Dublin
88 A2 **Portnoo** Donegl
85 E1 **Portraine** Dublin
83 E1 **Portroe** Tippry
89 D1 **Portrush** Antrim
89 D1 **Portstewart** Lderry
87 D4 **Portumna** Galway
82 C3 **Poulgorm Bridge** Kerry
89 D3 **Poyntz Pass** Armagh

R

85 D1 **Raharney** Wmeath
89 D2 **Randalstown** Antrim
89 D2 **Rasharkin** Antrim
85 D2 **Rathangan** Kildre
85 E2 **Rathcoole** Dublin
83 E3 **Rathcormack** Cork
84 C3 **Rathdowney** Laois
85 E2 **Rathdrum** Wicklw
89 D3 **Rathfriland** Down
83 D2 **Rathkeale** Limrck
88 B2 **Rathmelton** Donegl
82 C3 **Rathmore** Kerry
85 D1 **Rathmoylon** Meath
88 C1 **Rathmullan** Donegl
85 E2 **Rathnew** Wicklw
84 C1 **Rathowen** Wmeath
85 D3 **Rathvilly** Carlow
85 E1 **Ratoath** Meath
88 B2 **Ray** Donegl
86 B3 **Recess** Galway
86 B3 **Renvyle** Galway
83 E3 **Ringaskiddy** Cork
85 D3 **Ringville** Watfd
88 C4 **Rockcorry** Monhan
87 E2 **Roosky** Roscom
85 D4 **Rosbercon** Wexfd
87 D3 **Roscommon** Roscom
84 C2 **Roscrea** Tippry
88 B1 **Rosepenna** Donegl
83 D3 **Ross Carbery** Cork
87 D1 **Rosses Point** Sligo
85 E4 **Rosslare** Wexfd
85 E4 **Rosslare Harbour** Wexfd
88 C3 **Rosslea** Ferman
88 B3 **Rossnowlagh** Donegl

89 D4 **Rostrevor** Down
86 B3 **Roundstone** Galway
85 E2 **Roundwood** Wicklw
85 E1 **Rush** Dublin

89 E3 **Saintfield** Down
88 C2 **St Johnston** Donegl
85 D2 **Sallins** Kildre
86 C3 **Salthill** Galway
87 D4 **Scarriff** Clare
82 C2 **Scartaglin** Kerry
89 D3 **Scarva** Down
82 C4 **Schull** Cork
87 D2 **Scramoge** Roscom
88 C3 **Seskinore** Tyrone
83 E3 **Shanagarry** Cork
83 D1 **Shanagolden** Limrck
85 E2 **Shankill** Dublin
83 D1 **Shannon** Clare
87 D3 **Shannonbridge** Offaly
88 C4 **Shercock** Cavan
85 D3 **Shillelagh** Wicklw
84 C2 **Shinrone** Offaly
86 C3 **Shrule** Mayo
83 E1 **Silvermines** Tippry
88 C2 **Sion Mills** Tyrone
83 D1 **Sixmilebridge** Clare
85 E1 **Skerries** Dublin
82 C4 **Skibbereen** Cork
85 D1 **Slane** Meath
87 D1 **Sligo** Sligo
88 C3 **Smithborough**
     Monhan
82 B3 **Sneem** Kerry

82 C1 **Spanish Point** Clare
86 C3 **Spiddal** Galway
86 B3 **Sraith Salach** Galway
89 D3 **Stewartstown** Tyrone
85 E2 **Stillorgan** Dublin
85 D3 **Stonyford** Kilken
88 C2 **Strabane** Tyrone
85 D2 **Stradbally** Laois
88 C4 **Stradone** Cavan
85 D2 **Straffan** Kildre
87 D1 **Strandhill** Sligo
89 E3 **Strangford** Down
88 B2 **Stranorlar** Donegl
87 D2 **Strokestown** Roscom
85 D1 **Summerhill** Meath
88 B3 **Swanlinbar** Cavan
89 D2 **Swatragh** Lderry
86 C2 **Swinford** Mayo
85 E1 **Swords** Dublin

85 D4 **Taghmon** Wexfd
85 E4 **Tagoat** Wexfd
82 B3 **Tahilla** Kerry
85 E2 **Tallaght** Dublin
83 E3 **Tallow** Watfd
84 B4 **Tallowbridge** Watfd
89 D3 **Tandragee** Armagh
84 C1 **Tang** Wmeath
82 C1 **Tarbert** Kerry
84 C3 **Templemore** Tippry
84 C3 **Templetouhy** Tippry
89 D4 **Termonfeckin** Louth
85 D3 **Thomastown** Kilken
84 C3 **Thurles** Tippry

85 D2 **Timahoe** Laois
83 D3 **Timoleague** Cork
85 E3 **Tinahely** Wicklw
84 B3 **Tipperary** Tippry
87 D2 **Tobercurry** Sligo
89 D2 **Tobermore** Lderry
84 B3 **Toomyvara** Tippry
82 C4 **Toormore** Cork
82 C2 **Tralee** Kerry
85 D4 **Tramore** Watfd
85 D1 **Trim** Meath
86 C3 **Tuam** Galway
83 D1 **Tuamgraney** Clare
83 D1 **Tulla** Clare
84 C2 **Tullamore** Offaly
85 D3 **Tullow** Carlow
87 D2 **Tulsk** Roscom
86 C2 **Turlough** Mayo
84 C1 **Tyrellspass** Wmeath

84 C3 **Urlingford** Kilken

88 C4 **Virginia** Cavan

89 D4 **Warrenpoint** Down
85 D4 **Waterford** Watfd

83 E3 **Watergrasshill** Cork
82 B3 **Waterville** Kerry
86 C2 **Westport** Mayo
85 E4 **Wexford** Wexfd
83 E3 **Whitegate** Cork
89 E2 **Whitehead** Antrim
85 E2 **Wicklow** Wicklw
85 E3 **Woodenbridge**
     Wicklw
87 D4 **Woodford** Galway

83 E3 **Youghal** Cork